Simply Red

An Illustrated Biography by Mark Hodkinson

OMNIBUS PRESS

LONDON · NEW YORK · PARIS · SYDNEY

contents

In the café at lunch time; on the car radio during the drive home from work; at the shopping precinct on Saturday afternoon; in the pub that same evening - Mick Hucknall, his voice and his songs - everywhere.

The boy can sing, fact. This is where the consensus ends. He is a pariah to the music press, a plagiarist to the purist, but to millions of others his smooth voice sweetens the daily grind. His group's records, especially the phenomenal 'Stars', have propelled him to superstar status and made him a multi-millionaire.

He chinks glasses with the élite from the music, film, and sporting world and yet fans say they like him for his common touch. They think they see something real and authentic in his character. He sprang irresistibly from northern streets and astutely (ruthlessly?) found a path to glamour and wealth and fame and beautiful women. His mentor, manager Elliot Rashman, shaped and affixed himself to the same dream. They remain inseparable.

Simply Red or simply Mick? The latter, undoubtedly, especially now most of his original cohorts have been slipped quietly stage-left. No one has been allowed to dilute or tamper with a grand scheme which dates back to 1982 when Hucknall lived in a decrepit council flat and had to borrow money for food.

If you want, it can be an allegory of ambition - effort and self-belief overcoming innumerable difficulties and leading to success: the good guy winning in the end. Or, if you prefer, it is a victory for aggression and strength: the bad guy winning in the end.

If you want, it can also be merely a musical story. Hucknall would prefer it that way, he would rather we just listened. It can then be about exemplary musicianship and songwriting that has been honed to pop perfection.

chapter 1

The world was pretty much asleep in June of 1960. Plans to introduce colour televisions in the UK were dropped, hearing aids were issued on the NHS for the first time, British Somaliland became independent, Ingrid Bergman parted company with Roberto Rossellini: it was hardly worth turning the presses.

The Family Way

The Sixties would take some time yet to breathe into life. Carnaby Street was just another London walkway and the teenager, the British variety at any rate, waited impatiently for its invention.

On June 8, 1960, at St Mary's Hospital, among Manchester's bricks and bus stops, Michael James Hucknall was born to Reginald and Maureen Hucknall, his Christian names taken from his two grandfathers. The couple had married seven months earlier at Aspinall Methodist Church, Reddish, when Reg was 24 and Maureen about to turn 19.

They lived at first in a cramped flat at Bredbury near Stockport, but soon moved to Denton, a suburb of Manchester and one of a number of quasi-towns clinging roughly to the route of the River Tame. Dual carriageways now tear through the landscape but the brickworks, reservoirs, streets, industrial estates, lamp-posts and stray dogs are still there, on the other side of the hard shoulder. There is a town centre of sorts where shoe shops and supermarkets stand at the junction of Hyde Road and Stockport Road.

The Hucknall family home was in West Park Avenue, a mile or so south of the centre of Denton in an area known as Haughton Green which eventually meets the conurbation of Hyde. It is a long cul-de-sac of neat houses. There is no litter, people clean their cars on Sundays and front gardens are tended with care.

Reg Hucknall was a barber in Stockport. Vidal Sassoon had yet to bring his flamboyant touch to the trade - it was short back and sides all round at the shop where Reg worked. The customers read *Sporting Life* and the *Manchester Evening News* while they waited their turn. Reg, one of 11 children, was born in Barrow-in-Furness and had arrived in the Manchester area just a few years earlier after four years in the RAF.

'On June 8, 1960, at St Mary's Hospital, among Manchester's bricks and bus stops, Michael James Hucknall was born...'

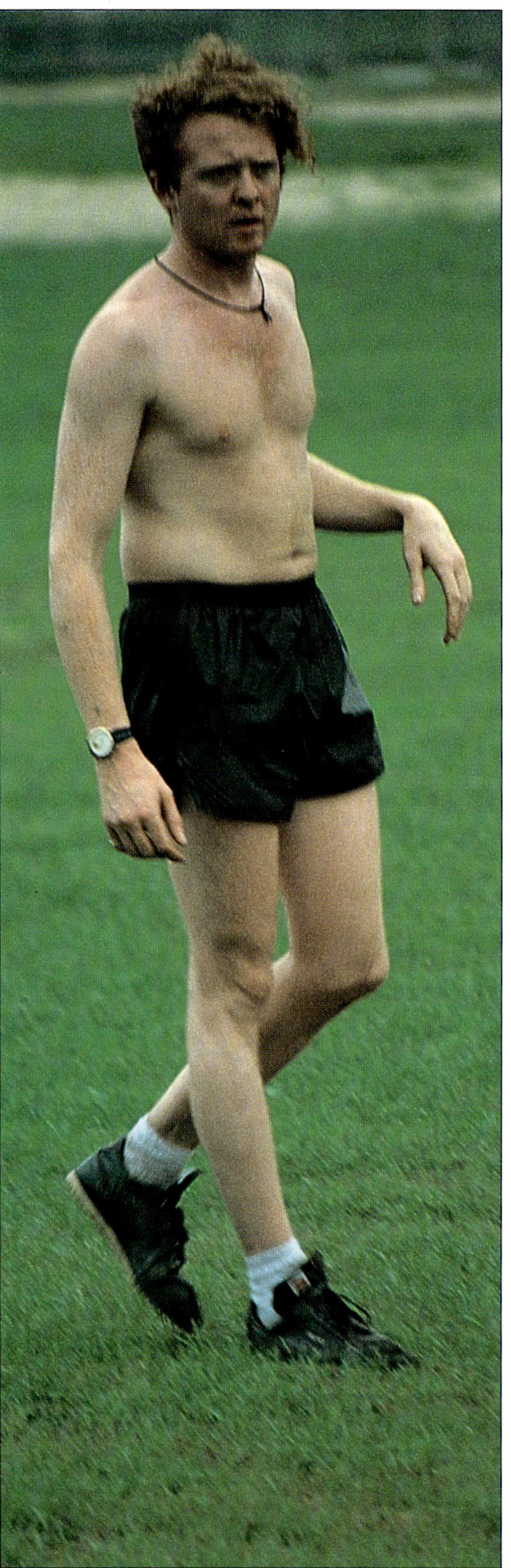

Maureen was from the small town of Penketh, where the Lancashire scenery of mills and valleys flattens out into the expansive fields of Cheshire and, eventually, the urbanised sprawl of Warrington. Her father, Michael Gibbons, was a mechanic who had travelled from Ireland to the mainland many years earlier and married a local girl called Florence.

The winter of 1963 was infamously cold. Newspapers tried to out-bid each other in a headline war. Towns were snowed in and water froze as it left the taps: perhaps it nearly was a 'White Hell'. It contrasted to the balmy summer of 1959 when Reg and Maureen first met The Hucknalls' marriage floundered against this white scenery and by Christmas 1963 Maureen was in lodgings with her three-year-old son. She was not suited to a life of domesticity, it made her old before her time. Some months before she left Reg, her younger sister, Marlene, had moved into the house and she watched enviously as she applied her make-up and went out for nights on the town. She was sometimes left alone with Michael because Reg attended greyhound meetings at the nearby Belle Vue stadium.

One evening Reg spotted her in a car with another man when he left the house to buy cigarettes. She claimed it was mistaken identity, but he was convinced. The gossips in West Park Avenue had expected as much. They had seen it coming, oh yes. Maureen was the stereotypical redhead; tempestuous and flighty. Poor Reg was quiet and easy-going, he deserved better.

Instinctively Maureen took her young son with her when she left the family home. They moved into a rented room on the other side of Denton and Maureen submitted herself to the unstructured life that existed before Reg Hucknall, and which pregnancy, marriage and a baby son had infringed. She worked during the day in Manchester as a typist and was reluctant to curtail her socialising in the evenings, sometimes leaving Michael with baby-sitters as young as 13.

Reg was allowed to visit on Friday evenings when he presented his estranged wife with money to keep Michael. They were doleful times for Reg, the weight fell off his frame as he pined for his son and the stability of before.

Members of Maureen's family were expected to help with the care of the child. On one occasion Marlene collected Michael from nursery and saw that his clothes were tatty and he had a persistent cough. She took him to her mother's, Florence Gibbons, who lived in the Cheshire village of Croft. He was there for just a few weeks before his grandmother decided that he should return to his father.

There was further turmoil during the following months as the child was passed from home to home but, after a bizarre scene in West Park Avenue when Michael was placed in three different sets of arms - his father's, his grandmother's and those of a neighbour called Nellie Spike, the decision was finally

'We're going to teach these people how to become soldiers and how to play rugger'.

made that he should remain with Reg. During this period Maureen went missing for weeks at a time and it was never seriously considered that he should pass into her care again.

Michael became known as Mick and attended Denton's St Lawrence's Primary School. The dissolution of his parents' marriage had no apparent effect on his personality. He was a boisterous, happy child; the loud ginger nut that almost everyone in the school knew. "His hair colour made him stand out a mile. He used to sing songs in the assembly hall at dinner time. I seem to remember him singing 'My Boy Lollipop'. He used to sing at the top of his voice," said a former classmate.

His father's sister, Sheila, was a Beatles' fanatic. Mick listened attentively when she played their records. At a family wedding he blasted out 'I Wanna Hold Your Hand' when he was six-years-old.

The maternal figure in his life was neighbour Nellie Spike, who had befriended Reg Hucknall. She had four daughters of her own and lived nearby with her husband, Alfred, in Manor Close. She collected Mick at the school gates and he remained with her until his father arrived home from work. She was known as 'Aunty Nellie' to Mick and would remain close to him all his life.

Mick was an intelligent pupil and unlike most of his friends he passed the Eleven Plus examination. A 'fail' would have meant that he attended Two Trees Secondary School which was literally over the garden fence, just a few hundred yards across a playing field. Instead, he had to take a bus ride down Stockport Road, through Denton, and on to the grammar school at nearby Audenshaw. The school ran parallel to a railway line, below the site of three huge reservoirs.

The demarcation between grammar and secondary modern schools was a strict educational tenet of British life in the Sixties. The grammar school pupils were the future middle-managers and teachers, the rest were the factory-hands and engineers. The warm ambience of aspiration chilled Hucknall. "I was always in trouble. Their attitude was, 'We're going to teach these people how to become soldiers and how to play rugger'. They tried to crush you. I despise any school that treats its kids like pet dogs instead of human beings," he said. The remark was made 15 years after leaving grammar school. The memory had lingered.

Friends noticed a marked change in his personality during his time at Audenshaw. He was lost amid the blazers and badges. He became sullen and introverted and unlike at primary school where he was generally liked, he was often mocked and ridiculed. A television advert running at the time featured a ventriloquist's dummy with red hair and freckles. Hucknall, inevitably, became 'Puppet Head' to members of the school rugby team. The nickname stuck for several months. Hucknall hated it.

He was a poor scholar and soon recognised that most of the other pupils had better academic qualities. He decided to opt out of a race he knew he could not win and became moody or disruptive in lessons, offering only flickering interest when it suited him. The few teachers who saw he had an inward intensity coaxed his enthusiasm and enjoyed his company. The majority, however, did not have the time and energy to bother. Physics teacher Dennis Martin, for instance, knew Hucknall spent most of his lessons drawing David Bowie album sleeves on his books and nothing, absolutely nothing, could imbue him with a love of flotation theories or light refraction.

Hucknall joined the school's army/airforce cadet troop. It was indicative of the type of school that it should have a military link based just 20 yards from the main school building. It was also, in 1992, one of the first schools in the area to 'opt-out' of local authority control under the new Conservative legislation.

Hucknall had been attracted to the cadet uniform and the prospect of missing the last lesson of the week, French. He did not attend again after receiving the trousers and jacket and was consequently court-martialled. The warning from the head of corps, Geoff Eastwood, was particularly stern: "You might be laughing now, but this will go down on your record and if there's another war and you're called up, you'll be in real trouble."

Girls from the school had mixed impressions of Hucknall. Some remembered him fondly as a sensitive, quiet, adolescent while others thought he was brash and vaguely odd. Physically he was neither ugly nor attractive, but he was certainly distinctive. He was loyal to the show business cliché and gushed with life when he was the centre of attention. At school discos his impression of Gary Glitter was a delight. The other lads tried to mimic the crazed histrionics of the singer, but none carried it off with the same aplomb as Hucknall.

'You might be laughing now, but this will go down on your record...'

There were girls willing to share hurried clinches with Hucknall in dark corners after school and in the church yard at St Lawrence's. His sexual development - stuttered, awkward, emboldened by illicit gulps of cider and sherry, painful crushes, rejection, fumbling hands - was perfectly normal. Reg Hucknall was pleased, it had been a secret fear that the unusual circumstances of his son's home environment (for the times at least) might lead him to homosexuality.

He fell in with a roguish gang and stole lead from roofs, including St Lawrence's, and inflicted himself with a home-made tattoo on his arm. He drank heavily and for someone so young he quickly embraced a lifestyle of nightclubs, fist-fights, pool tables, football matches and girls.

The cadet troop building next to Audenshaw Grammar School.

On a week's holiday to Butlin's in Ayr soon after his sixteenth birthday, Hucknall met a Scottish girl and they spent the night together in the chalet he was sharing with friends. It was the beginning of what was to become a celebrated, colourful sexual career.

Unsurprisingly, in the summer of 1976, he did not gain good results in the school exams. He failed to show for mathematics and physics and received an unclassified mark for geography and English literature. The sum total of a schooling deemed to have been privileged was three O-levels; 'C' grades in art and English language and a 'B' in economics.

The estrangement of Reg and his son from Maureen Hucknall and her family was total. Florence Gibbons had only a small photograph of the boy she called 'Our Michael' and had watched the colours fade from the picture down the years. No contact was made during his childhood; she said she was warned off by Nellie Spike. Reg Hucknall had destroyed all the photographs of himself with his former wife and had flushed his wedding ring down the toilet.

Maureen Hucknall's life did not have the tranquillity of the family she had left behind in Denton. She pursued a single-minded, enigmatic course, walking in and out of people's lives, frequently leaving pain and distress in her wake. It would later be suggested that there were parallels with her son's musical career.

Soon after leaving Reg she fell hopelessly in love with an engineer 16 years her senior, Austrian-born Imre Kozarits. Although he considered himself indifferent to her charms, Kozarits was soon lending her money to cover the rent for her room in Whalley Range. She persuaded him to abandon plans to emigrate to Canada and, almost by a process of sweet seduction, within weeks he found himself living with her in another flat, this time in Chorlton. A few weeks went by before she calmly told Kozarits some information she had previously kept from him: she was married and had a small child.

He was deeply upset to learn that he was implicated in the break-up of a marriage. He, in uncharacteristic forcefulness, ordered that she return to her husband and child. Coyly, with tears in her eyes, she said that it was not possible: she was pregnant with *his* child. He immediately offered to stand by her. He later realised that he had again fallen for her duplicity when their first child, Ricky, was born more than nine months after the announcement of her 'pregnancy'.

Maureen had access to her son for a short period and they spent Saturdays together with Kozarits, whom Hucknall called 'Jim' because he had difficulty saying Imre. Her new husband looked forward to the visits, he liked the youngster's liveliness and watched in amazement as he sat bewitched in front of the television when the pop programme *The Six Five Special* was broadcast. He thought Maureen's attitude to Mick was peculiar, she appeared not to care that her life was being lived largely separate from his. The subject was never covered in depth because Kozarits was wary of his wife's keen temper.

The couple had another child three years later, a girl called Lyndsey. When Lyndsey was just one-year-old, Maureen left Imre in pitiful circumstances. She took her daughter while Kozarits was out with Ricky and moved in with another man. Some weeks later she contacted her husband and said she would hand Lyndsey back at a police station in the Midlands. While she was severing her ties with Kozarits, news filtered through that her divorce from Reg Hucknall was finally complete - with Kozarits cited for adultery.

Maureen saw her daughter intermittently but after her sixth birthday they were separated for 11 years. In the meantime, Maureen had married Danish seaman Renee Simonsen and had another two children, Michaela and Alan. This marriage also broke up and early in 1992 she took her fourth husband, a businessman from Texas.

R & VAN HIRE
R LIVERPOOL RD

Hucknall had no idea of his mother's whereabouts or activities during his childhood. His world was built around his doting father, Aunty Nellie and her daughters, and friends from school and the neighbourhood. In such circumstances it was inevitable that he would forge a strong bond with his father. "Dad is the person I admire. He was the one who did all the hard work when I needed it, the one who brought me up, and the one I now care about and love. From the day my mother walked out he has refused to say a bad word about her," he said.

He had no desire to trace his mother or her side of the family. It was not until he was a famous 32-year-old singing millionaire that he became fully aware of his extended family. As a teenager he had told inquisitive friends and neighbours that he did not care about his mother or ever want to see her. It was obvious, then, that by 1992 it was far too late to develop a worthwhile relationship with them. Besides, he was determined not to hurt his father's feelings.

In the space of a few days in July 1992 he read in the tabloid press about his mother's family. He must have expected the news to arrive at any time considering his fame. He discovered that he had a half-sister, Lyndsey Kozarits, and half-brother, Ricky Kozarits. Lyndsey, by coincidence a Simply Red fan, had curly red hair tumbling to her shoulders and the same small, flat eyes as Hucknall.

Lyndsey revealed that her mother had contacted Hucknall five years earlier. "He told her that he had nothing to say to her, that he didn't know her or what she looked like. He said he had had such a good childhood without her and didn't want to know her now," she said. Maureen's telephone call, their first communication in nearly 20 years, had quickly evolved into an argument and Maureen slammed down the phone in fury. Florence Gibbons saw the irony of two people with similarly strong, bloody-minded characters immediately reaching an impasse. They were, for a few seconds at least, mother and son: not that it really mattered.

Reg Hucknall reacted with typical pragmatism when he learned of the bid for reconciliation. "She's got a bloody nerve," he told pressmen. "Talk about a face from the past. If she hadn't bothered about us for the past 20 odd years, why now? She knew where we lived. I was pleased that Mick disowned her, although I didn't tell him that at the time. I didn't want to influence him in any way."

Lyndsey, unlike Hucknall, had agreed to meet her mother again after the long separation. "There are always two sides to every story. The first thing I asked her when she came through the door was why she had left me. Now I see her as a free spirit. She has enjoyed her life and you've got to admire her for that," she said.

Perhaps Hucknall's mother would have had a more positive response if she had contacted her son a decade earlier.

The lyrics to 'Holding Back The Years' give, if taken literally, a clear indication of his feelings at that time - 'Hoping for the arms of mater, got to meet her sooner or later.' The feeling had obviously dissipated since the late Seventies when the song was written.

There were more family members ready to pour their lament into a reporter's notepad. Florence Gibbons, then 73, was next to speak. 'I Mourn For Mick As If He Was Dead' was the headline in *The Sun*. The paper's reporter, Peter Willis, spoke to her late at night over the telephone. She had waited years to talk about her grandson: "Michael will always be the little boy I lost. I know I have lost him for good." It was all Aunty Nellie's fault: "She wrote me a terrible letter saying I had been a bad mother, with all my children leaving home, and telling me to leave Michael alone," she said.

Willis had picked his moment well, it was good copy. "I remember crying when I saw him for the first time on TV. I was so excited. The next day I went out and bought his first LP. I couldn't understand some of it but I was in tears listening," said Florence.

'I remember crying when I saw him for the first time on TV. I was so excited...'

Florence Gibbons had met Hucknall backstage after a concert at London's Brixton Academy four years earlier. The sight of an old woman clutching a programme and asking for Hucknall's autograph had prompted a member of the security staff to direct her through to the VIP room. "When Michael came in with his band I asked him for his autograph. He said: 'Yes, of course, who are you?' You should have seen his expression when I replied: 'I'm your grandma'."

Their time together was brief but she said he treated her 'like a lady'. Hucknall was later dismissive: "I remember this woman coming up and saying she was my grandma, and to be honest, I felt nothing. It was weird, but I felt nothing at all. But why should I? Why should they want to get in contact now?"

Reg Hucknall believed the sudden flurry of relatives keen to befriend Hucknall was down to his fame; they wanted to feel its glow. The Kozarits were upset because they felt the press had treated them unfairly. "This bloke came to interview us and said he was writing a book about Simply Red. We didn't know he was from the paper until the next day when it was in *The Sun*," complained Ricky Kozarits. He did not recognise the family portrayed in the paper, desperate for Hucknall's recognition. "It ruined any chance we had of meeting him. The whole thing caused us a lot of upset," he said. Willis, *The Sun*'s reporter, denied that he had secured the story through illicit means.

Four months after leaving grammar school Hucknall began a two-year arts course at Tameside College of Further Education in Ashton-under-Lyne, a few miles east of Denton. The move coincided with his first involvement in pop groups. Punk was about to galvanise the British music scene but in the meantime bands which would later be termed 'heavy rock' were the chief influence on young musicians.

The Beatles were still Hucknall's favourite band. He played their records so often that he could recognise a particular track by the grooves in the vinyl. Some friends had formed a band called Osiris, named after the chief Egyptian deity, the god who brought civil order to Egypt, no less. The name, typically, had been discovered on a school trip to an exhibition at Manchester University.

Hucknall took over as singer and was pleased to belt out faithful copies of rock songs by the likes of Cream, Deep Purple, Free, The Rolling Stones and Hawkwind. He was drawn to the quiet guitarist, Neil Moss, who he had known during their time together at St Lawrence's. He had more musical intuition than the rest and was happy to spend hours working out chords with Hucknall. Moss had also passed his Eleven Plus but refused to leave his friends behind and instead moved with them to Two Trees Secondary Modern. They both idolised The Beatles and began writing songs together. They were going to be musical craftsmen, the new Lennon and McCartney.

A weekend job collecting beer glasses at Denton's Broomstairs Working Men's Club gave Hucknall easy access to alcohol and he was fast developing a taste for it, 10 pints were sometimes downed during the course of an evening. The heavy drinking, under-age too, led to rows with his father. On a more positive note, he was able to secure a rehearsal room above the club.

Osiris had just one song of their own by their first concert, a gentle number with lyrics by Hucknall called 'Time Over Matter'. The concert in December 1976 was at a Methodist church hall in Denton and was part of an evening's entertainment for the local swimming club, Onward Dolphins. There was no proper stage, the plug was pulled before they completed their set, but generally it was a success. Hucknall certainly enjoyed himself.

Their next concert was two months later at the Working Men's Club where they practised. There was a poignant vignette of the future Hucknall. Some college friends were milling around backstage before the performance and Hucknall insisted that they left; the group needed a few minutes of hushed contemplation. It was remarkably pretentious, but no one had the nerve to tell Hucknall.

The band drifted apart but Moss and Hucknall were inseparable. Aside from writing and playing music together, they were always by each other's side. Hucknall, for a short period, joined a sub-heavy metal band without Moss called Joe Stalin's Red Star Radio Band and sang for a while with another rock band called Purple Haze, but otherwise all his musical projects for the next six years were to involve Moss.

Punk finally arrived in 1976. The Sex Pistols played twice in Manchester within a few weeks at the Lesser Free Trade Hall and after the second performance on July 20, 1976, legend has it that the audience, en bloc, of which Hucknall was one, bought either a microphone or guitar and formed a punk band the next morning. Clubs like the Electric Circus in Collyhurst were soon hosting nights of burning plectrums and three chord pile-ups as touring bands passed through. The local scene was changed irrevocably and volunteered its own wave of guitar upstarts with The Buzzcocks at its forefront.

Hucknall and Moss were there, impressed by the energy and the attitude and the rebellion. They wanted it all, but only on condition that their songs had a melody; they could not eschew the Lennon/McCartney legacy, it would be sacrilege. Their very first song was a number called 'Marion'.

There was another element thrown into the bizarre mixture - Hucknall's love of art. It had been his favourite subject at school and, much like music, it was a focus for his expression and aggression. At college in Tameside he was no more than an average student but he excelled in the mixed media classes held by the lecturer, Mike Rooke. Students were encouraged to dance, sing, make music and videos - it was the only time during the week when Hucknall was really alive and the vitality was tangible. "You could sense the enthusiasm welling up within him as our sessions began," said Rooke.

During these sessions Hucknall, along with three others, wrote and sang one of his own songs, before putting it on to tape as an illustration for the class project on the nature of commercial culture. Sadly, the track, possibly Hucknall's first to be recorded, was erased.

Another time, Rooke held a 'happening' and encouraged the class to stage a piece of performance art. Hucknall went further than the rest, climbing out of a two-storey window, across a thin ledge, and back into the classroom through another window. The withdrawn, often-bullied Hucknall of before had all but vanished. Punk had given him self-esteem and he was frequently arrogant and callous. He dismissed some of the other pupils' work as 'shit' and did not care that it might cause upset. It was only his view, they could have a similar one of his work, what was the fuss?

A reluctant bass player, Mark Reeder, joined in rehearsals with the pair. He was a college friend of Hucknall's and had excellent connections through his job at Virgin Records in Manchester. It was a musical crossover period from rock to punk for most but their newly-appointed drummer, Steve Tansley, had not started the journey. Before taking the drum stool he would carefully fold his afghan coat and part his curtain of hair. Hucknall's own adoption of punk was made almost as hesitatingly. He still played, and enjoyed, records that

'You could sense the enthusiasm welling up within him as our sessions began'.

were mildly progressive, but while on holiday at his cousins' in Barrow-in-Furness, he cut and spiked his hair properly.

Typically, when he did 'go punk' everyone had to know. It was no coincidence that a laughing, screaming Hucknall was pogoing at the front of The Clash's concert at Belle Vue's Elizabethan Suite a few months afterwards. Hucknall had seen the cameras from Granada Television scanning the stage and first few rows. It was a chance not to be missed. The camera shot depicting his joyous abandonment was the perfect freeze-frame of the 16-year-old Hucknall: delirious, reckless, and most importantly, somewhere near the front.

Hucknall, Moss, Reeder and Tansley became The Frantic Elevators. The name, much like the music, was simultaneously abstruse, humorous and possibly artistic. Originally they were to be known as Elevation after the Television song but a headline in *NME* containing the word 'Frantic' had drawn their attention and the name was re-arranged to accommodate it. They continued to rehearse at Broadstairs Working Men's Club. Reeder's contacts served them well and their début concert was as support to Bethnal at Rafters club in the city centre.

"The material was jerky and quirky. A lot of songs had swearing in them [in rehearsal they used to perform a number called 'Fuck Off'], I don't know if it was done for effect. There were no germs of greatness but they had a sound of their own and the set did not blur into one like it does with a lot of bands. They were certainly tighter than most bands around at that time," said one observer.

Neil Moss' older brother, Ian, was himself involved in the scene, playing in various groups. He watched with interest as Hucknall and his brother developed their musical bond. "Mick was always very enthusiastic about music, he had an unqualified love of it. He always put it before any social considerations. Perhaps Neil was not quite as keen but when it evolved into The Frantic Elevators it became a quest. There was almost a religious fervour about it and they were very, very committed. They rehearsed on Christmas Day for a few years, it was like a statement of how much it meant to them," he said.

The band with a reluctant bassist (Reeder had plans to emigrate to Germany) found a reluctant manager. Pete Dervin, a friend with a settled address and telephone, found himself accidentally qualified to do the job. He was handed a pile of business cards with 'Frantic Elevators Management' printed on them with his name and number beneath. He was flattered and accepted a role he had not solicited without complaint.

The band found a new rehearsal base at a former warehouse in Little Peter Street, very close to where the city's Boardwalk Club was later established. The rehearsal rooms were also used by other Manchester luminaries, some, like The Buzzcocks, famous, and others, like Ed Banger and The Nosebleeds, merely whimsical ideas fleshed out. It was run by Tony Davidson, the son of a Manchester jeweller. He was initially a Northern Soul fan but found his premises patronised by itchy guitar bands branding themselves New Wave. "The idea of running the practice studios was to get a free flow of talent coming through. The next thing to do was get involved with some of the bands," he said.

Davidson formed TJM Records. The beast of corporate rock was asleep and the UK was awash with bands, labels, promoters, artists and writers, all plying their trade from backbedrooms. Manchester already had its share of record labels - Rabid, Absurd, Groovy, Illuminated, Streets Ahead, Object Music and, of course, Factory. The confidence and vision of Factory was unique and it meant that the others were unfairly

viewed as corner shop and mundane. There was, in fact, life outside the portals of the Factory empire, even if it was sometimes hesitant and unsure of itself.

The first release on TJM was V2's 'Man In The Box'. V2, from Gorton (not Dublin!), were a failed attempt to merge The New York Dolls with David Bowie. Their bedizened image, and their first record, was greeted by deafening apathy. The label's second release, 'You're Not Going Out Like That' by The Distractions was made 'single of the week' in *Sounds*. Davidson was already forming plans to release a record by The Frantic Elevators. "The piercing vocals were the first thing that caught my imagination. This prompted me to sign the band to my label," he said.

Mark Reeder finally left the group before any recorded work could be released. His place was taken by Brian Turner, another student at Tameside and an old friend of Hucknall's. He was a novice on bass guitar but had a warm, humorous personality which the others liked.

'They rehearsed on Christmas Day for a few years, it was like a statement of how much it meant to them'.

chapter 2

In London a 53-year-old woman with white-yellow hair held up her hands in glee. She leaned forward on the staircase to get closer to the microphones and cameras. "Where there is discord may we bring harmony, where there is despair may we bring hope." A party researcher had found the quote in a biography of St. Francis of Assisi. One hundred and eighty five miles up the motorway, 18-year-old Mick Hucknall was in Manchester, pulling his band's first ever record from cardboard boxes.

Liverpool's Finest

May 1979, the timing was poignant: the last days of Socialist rule in the UK and the election of Margaret Thatcher. It was also the start of Mick Hucknall's recording career. He would, in the years to come, rant against Conservative ideology but the calendar would always mock: Hucknall and Thatcher, simply red and simply blue.

The change of government was inevitable. The winter of 1978/79 was so bleak the media modified the title of a John Steinbeck book as its catch phrase - 'The Winter of Discontent'. The bakers went on strike in November and in the New Year they were joined by the lorry drivers, railway workers, civil servants, and by the middle of January even grave-diggers had downed their shovels. The buses in Manchester were taken off the road when lorry drivers refused to deliver fuel. Mick Hucknall and his group had to walk to rehearsals. Tony Davidson had noticed that Hucknall was forever stalking the corridors of his dingy premises and other bands joked that he

The Frantic Elevators
(Left to Right) Brian Turner,
Kevin Williams, Neil Moss,
Mick Hucknall.

didn't seem to have a home to go to. It was early evidence of an unusual dedication.

The group had a new member behind the drum kit, Kevin Williams, who worked at a printers close to the rehearsal rooms and lived a few miles down Oldham Road in Chadderton. Tansley had left because he was tired of rehearsing endlessly, often the same song for hours, and he believed his rhythm section partner, Brian Turner, just wasn't up to the job. Davidson had recommended Williams and the first concert of what was to become a stable Frantic Elevators line-up of Hucknall, Moss, Turner and Williams was in the summer of 1979 at Manchester's Band On The Wall club.

City Fun was an irreverent magazine glued together and stapled down by prime movers with pseudonyms like Andy Zero and Martin X. A postcard from Alternative Manchester, *City Fun* could justifiably boast that a band did not exist officially until it had been mentioned within its pages. The logo of the city's established newspaper, the *Manchester Evening News*, was 'A Friend Dropping In'; *City Fun's* was, 'A Friend Dropping Out', and contributors could use bad language - while punctuation and spelling were arbitrary.

Issue seven of *City Fun* was devoted largely to the release of The Fall's début album, 'Live At The Witch Trials'. Other Manchester bands in the paper's roll call included The Distractions, The Smirks, The Hamsters, Armed Force, The Drones and The Cheeters. Joy Division received a mention that was eerily prophetic. 'I can't put up with their writhing singer for too long,' wrote 'Nicky'.

Hucknall was desperate to release a record. His taste was already varied and his love of The Beatles and punk was tempered with a fondness for soul and rhythm and blues. He could sing from memory every song on The Rolling Stones' 'Sticky Fingers' album. He knew also of Davidson's enthusiasm for soul, he had adapted the inner label design for TJM from an old soul record. Cleverly, Hucknall suggested that the band's début should be a cover of a classic soul record. It was a bad idea, it was not cool for New Wave groups to even concede that soul music existed.

The Frantic Elevators' début single, of which 2,000 were pressed, was 'Voice In The Dark' b/w 'Passion' and 'Every Day I Die', recorded for £600 in a small studio in Chorlton. It was reviewed by Andy Zero in *City Fun*. Before concluding that the aggregate of the three songs was, 'A good record', he referred to, 'A clean sound with a catchy riff and crisp drums underpinned by the bass. The lyrics, as on all these songs, concern themselves with an aspect of sex'.

The review was cursory, stuck at the bottom of a column. The band's name was written by hand, as if its inclusion was an afterthought. Even on the comparatively small Manchester scene, The Frantic Elevators were not seen as anything important.

A copy of the record reached *Melody Maker* and its response was damning: 'TJM specialise in records that are completely unremarkable. The B-side, 'Every Day I Die' is a moronic noise. It is putridly abysmal. Excuse me while I grab my plastic bag.'

Radio One's John Peel, who had earlier dismissed one of the band's demo tapes, played the single regularly on his show. TJM's distribution network was shambolic and amounted to Davidson and a friend calling shops directly and asking them to place orders. Mick Middles, a Manchester stringer for *Sounds*, encouraged the paper to include the single in its independents chart. It was placed at number eight in a chart which reflected journalists' current talked-about bands rather than sales.

It was, even for its time, a fragile and insignificant record. The main track was a jaunty ditty clinging desperately to fuzz guitar and basic drumming. The backing vocals sounded like a pub sing-song after last orders and the one string guitar solo veered close to a Buzzcocks' parody. Hucknall's voice, the celebrated honey pot of resonance and control, was a reedy and nondescript impression of a bored teenager, nothing more. Friends of the group were surprised at their choice of 'Voice In The Dark' because they felt there were stronger songs in their set.

'Passion' and 'Every Day I Die' were at least vaguely experimental and short, at 55 seconds and one minute 20 seconds respectively. 'Passion' began with a Joy Division-patented bass line before Hucknall's arrival in syncopation with a drum beat, singing quickly-very-quickly. The other song owed much to the fascination at the time of robotic beats and featured just Hucknall and a droning backing vocal against a repetitive drum rhythm. On the record Neil Moss was credited as Neil Smith to avoid investigation by the dole office.

The songs should really have remained on a demo tape to procure the odd gig but the post-punk spirit of spontaneity meant that flaws and naïvety were often framed on seven inches of plastic. It was a highly inauspicious début and the only theme to remain constant and be developed was in the lyric of 'Voice In The Dark' when Hucknall sang, 'Everything swirls around me.'

The band found a new 'manager' when Richard Watt moved into a flat in Hulme with Brian Turner. Pete Dervin was happy to relinquish his position, although Watt was more of an enthusiastic friend than real management material. He was keen on photography and accompanied the band to concerts, at first simply to take pictures but later working on their behalf. At this time the group members, including Hucknall, had re-located to Hulme flats, grey slabs of concrete skirting the edge of the city centre, infested with cockroaches and criminals.

'It is putridly abysmal. Excuse me while I grab my plastic bag'.

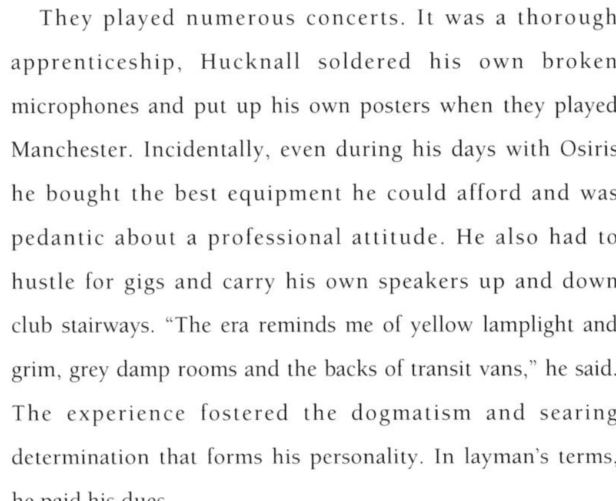

'In my first year I was a nutcase. I had most of my hair shaved off and would not talk to anybody'.

They played numerous concerts. It was a thorough apprenticeship, Hucknall soldered his own broken microphones and put up his own posters when they played Manchester. Incidentally, even during his days with Osiris he bought the best equipment he could afford and was pedantic about a professional attitude. He also had to hustle for gigs and carry his own speakers up and down club stairways. "The era reminds me of yellow lamplight and grim, grey damp rooms and the backs of transit vans," he said. The experience fostered the dogmatism and searing determination that forms his personality. In layman's terms, he paid his dues.

He was not a Boy Genius in the mould of Stevie Wonder, Steve Winwood, Prince, or even George Michael; his talent was based on graft and discipline. He was precocious rather than skilled. He had the ideas and the vision and the gall. It was some time later before he realised he was blessed with an unusually expressive voice. In the meantime, he was happy at the front, showing off, shouting off and getting up a few noses.

He developed a method of writing songs with Moss in a style commonly adopted by many singer songwriters with limited instrumental skills, and it was a method he would utilise throughout his career. He could play basic chords on the guitar and would strum them as backing for his own vocal melodies. He sometimes played rhythm guitar on stage and was proficient enough to scratch out the backbone of a song. He relied on the various members of his group to interpret his songwriting ideas and suggest how chords might best fit together, but the heart of songs, especially later on, came from Hucknall himself; indeed, they benefited substantially from the simplistic brilliance that comes from an intuitive musician as opposed to a virtuoso.

Tony Davidson organised a package tour of artists on the roster and issued a compilation album called 'Identity Parade'. The Frantic Elevators did not appear on the record but were to play live alongside V2, The Distractions, Private Sector and The Pathetics in towns off the regular circuit like Oldham, Middlesbrough and Wakefield. Davidson slogged away thanklessly for weeks but, unlike the successful Stiff Tour of 1979 on which it was roughly based, it did not have the depth of talent or a suitably large promotional budget. It was, for all his efforts, strictly small-time and several promoters pulled out of scheduled shows.

Although he was rightly to claim some part in the discovery of Mick Hucknall, Davidson was at this point championing V2. "The tour was for the benefit of V2. There was a minor payola where Tony would give the DJ a couple of quid to play V2 songs during the evening, supposedly to build up hysteria in the crowd for when they played. The Frantic Elevators, in

The Frantic Elevators were not different enough to stand out from the crowd. There were hundreds of other groups a grade up from pub rock, throwing tantrums around a drums, bass, guitar format - and many had more flair than they had. They wore jeans and sweaters and apart from Hucknall, who held a vestige of style, they looked more like plumbers than trainee rock stars. In fact, Turner was a time-served electrician while Williams was married with a child and still working as a printer.

The record encouraged the band, however, and Hucknall began to develop an on-stage charisma. There was little of the sneer refined by other Manchester bands like The Fall; Hucknall was generally warm, endearing and had nerve. He invited members of the audience to play percussion and if there was a need to lighten the evening he would impersonate Joy Division's Ian Curtis or rip through The Clash's 'White Riot'. The voice was also being noticed. "As a compliment to their ability, I vividly remember a particular venue, the Rock Garden in Middlesbrough, where 700 punks stopped their ritual spitting to listen to their full set," said Davidson.

Tony's eyes, were a support band for V2. It did not undermine them, they were sure of their own ability. I think it irritated them, particularly because they thought V2 were awful," said one musician. Davidson denied that there was any confusion over priorities. "It soon became obvious that Hucknall was the real star. Everybody on that tour, whether they cared to admit it or not, recognised Hucknall's star quality," he said.

Three more songs were recorded by The Frantic Elevators with a view to releasing another single on TJM - 'The Hunchback Of Notre Dame', 'See Nothing And Everything' and 'Don't Judge Me'. Twenty white labels were pressed but it was not given an official release because Davidson was having proverbial cash-flow problems. Before recording the three songs, Hucknall had asked Davidson to consider releasing the ballad 'Holding Back The Years' but Davidson said, quite simply, that it was not strong enough.

The aborted single showed that they had not progressed greatly. Hucknall's accentuated Manchester drawl on the main track was not dissimilar to Jilted John who had scored a novelty hit in July 1978 on another Manchester label, Rabid. 'See Nothing And Everything' was a controlled punk song, but again there was no evidence that they had learned to exploit their one real asset, Hucknall's voice. He finally got a chance to sing properly on 'Don't Judge Me', a twee number that ripped into chaotic feedback via more hesitant drum rolls. The Frantic Elevators were still clearly a confounding force.

Davidson was busy with other projects. Slaughter and The Dogs had a reasonable profile through spirited if one-dimensional releases on Rabid and Decca Records. They were welcomed enthusiastically at TJM where Davidson referred to them as 'very talented boys' when he spoke to Hucknall. "He saw Slaughter and The Dogs as his step into the big time. They'd soon been sussed out by everyone, except Tony," said an insider.

Hucknall completed the course at Tameside and began a degree course in Fine Art at Manchester Polytechnic. He liked the atmosphere: "College was completely different to school, they were really concerned with treating you like an adult. They earned your respect and I respected them," said Hucknall. One of his fellow students referred to his time at the Polytechnic as, 'A piss-up, a three year holiday!'

At Tameside he had marked himself out as an individual. He briefly wore a dog collar and his bright clothes made him conspicuous against Denton's drab streets. He was occasionally set upon and revelled in the renegade image: an orange jacket, a black eye, a ripped T-shirt, anything that made him stand out was cherished. "In my first year I was a nutcase. I had most of my hair shaved off and would not talk to anybody."

The tutors encouraged students to veer from figurative work but he refused. He continually drew his bicycle and worked diligently on a picture that was composed merely of the word 'Fuck' written many times. He eventually smashed it up and absented himself from lectures for a week. He was, despite the occasional exhibitionism, remembered fondly by staff. "He was a very happy-go-lucky kind of person. Something of a joker, very popular, what you might call a campus personality. I always remember him wearing a big black hat," said David Hensler, the head of department.

During the course Hucknall developed a cubist approach, influenced by Picasso. Painting was always his second love though: "I was always a better singer than I was a painter. Painting is hard work. I had to try and think and think and think whereas with music it seemed to come naturally. I thought that I shouldn't really be labouring at something, I should do something that's natural to me and that's why I ended up doing music," he explained.

He maintained his shock tactics until the end, collecting his 2:2 degree at the graduation ceremony wearing a bright woolly jumper and trousers while the rest were attired in suits.

There was, at last, a small celebration in the life of The Frantic Elevators. They forced themselves on to the bill for a three-day rock festival called Futurama at Leeds Queens Hall in September 1980. The élite of UK's New Wave bands appeared - Public Image, Joy Division, Soft Cell, Scritti Politti, Young Marble Giants, Altered Images - and it was a chance for upstarts like The Frantic Elevators to appear before a large crowd, albeit as one of the first bands to play. The band, apart from a sloppy version of 'Production Prevention', played the gig of their life. It was no surprise when the group's only song broadcast on Granada's hour-long programme dedicated to the festival was 'Production Prevention'; it had, somehow, been inevitable.

In the spirit of independent labels, TJM faltered at the end of 1980. *City Fun* reported in December that Davidson was to appear in court for non-payment of rent on his rehearsal studios. He was ordered to pay the outstanding £4,000 at £15 per week. There was also reference to a court case involving Davidson and one of his bands, The Distractions. It was alleged that he owed them £250 as settlement of their court costs.

Although songs recorded for TJM were released in 1987 as a mini-LP of vintage Mick Hucknall material, on the day it closed early in 1981 its legacy was eight singles, four EPs, three aborted singles, one compilation album... and the début of a talent to later sell more than 20 million records throughout the world.

Hucknall and Moss continued writing songs - more than 50 by the middle of 1980 - oblivious to when, if ever, they might be released on vinyl. They were learning their craft. "There's a lot of water under the bridge between me and Neil and I think we learned a lot of song writing techniques together. There's so much I learned, not from Neil particularly, but while we were together," said Hucknall.

Eventually, The Frantic Elevators would be seen as a minor diversion in Hucknall's life before the real business of Simply Red started. In truth Hucknall was deadly earnest about his first serious group. He wrote a letter to the *Sounds* journalist, Johnny Waller, early in 1980. The sentiment was intense: 'The band will never give up, because we all know what we want from it all, and it's mainly the best music we can make. If after this explanation you think we're making a mistake or something, then that's OK with me. If you want to do a review in *Sounds* for us then that's alright too.' The letter was cool; a playful mixture of confidence and aggression. He desperately wanted the review, but he cleverly made it appear as if he was indifferent to the idea. Already he was adept at the art of manipulation.

Waller had seen the band when they were third on the bill supporting Slaughter and The Dogs at Manchester's Russell Club two years earlier. He was impressed by their defiance - the punk audience had wanted amphetamine noise but they defiantly ran through their eccentric stop-start pop. "I thought they were fun and really funny. On one hand they were awful, kind of amateurish, but at the same time Mick had a kind of charisma," he said.

Hucknall got his feature article and on January 17, 1981, his cherubic face peered from the pages of *Sounds*. He was, naturally, at the front: a James Dean shrug, hands-in-pocket, thick Aran sweater, hair immaculate. The others assembled behind him - awkward poses, Christmas jumpers, hairstyles grown out months earlier. They might have been workmen fixing Hucknall's roof, having their picture taken during a tea break.

Waller remembered interviewing Hucknall in a 'small pokey house' (probably his father's) and staying up most of the night. "He was pushy, he was determined, but Mick was always really down to earth. Some people just have this determination. Mick was never so steely-eyed that you thought, 'Oh my God, here's someone destined for success'. He was jokey and jovial, I think in many ways it stopped people taking him seriously. He was somebody like a hundred other cocky lead singers with bands that I interviewed. He was a mixture of aggression and laddish mateyness."

The journalist was surprised to find Moss strumming the chords to The Beatles 'I'm So Tired' and Neil Young's 'Heart of

'I was always a better singer than I was a painter. Painting is hard work...'

Gold'. "Good music always wins through in the end," explained Hucknall. The article immediately marked the group out as terminally unfashionable in music press terms. They wanted hit singles, for a start. "I'd like hit singles, yeah, and I think anybody who doesn't must be an idiot, must be a clown - to wrap themselves up in the aesthetics that aren't important to music. It would be very nice to have a hit, yeah," he said.

The live scene was relatively buoyant in the early Eighties. Punk had regenerated small venues and people were back into the habit of hearing music in an intimate setting. The Frantic Elevators, with comical irony in hindsight, appeared alongside nine other Manchester bands at the 'Stuff the Superstars' festival at the Mayflower in July 1980. Despite numerous concerts in their home city, The Frantic Elevators could not establish a following. "For some reason, we've never managed to get anywhere with an audience in Manchester, not once. I find it strange - because I can't understand why. Sometimes we've been brilliant in Manchester and got nothing - we've also been very bad," said Neil Moss at the time.

The musical hierarchy in Manchester disapproved of The Frantic Elevators. The city's tight musical clique eulogised the puritanical values epitomised by Joy Division/New Order. The expressions were blank, the clothes drab, smiling was uncool; there was precious communication between audience and band and no one admitted that they craved fame. "The Elevators were absolutely vilified in Manchester. There was a real sense of community in the city but they felt miles apart from it. They were seen as uncool," said one musician.

Surprisingly, The Frantic Elevators built up a quasi-friendship with members of The Fall after playing concerts together. It seemed as if arch maverick Mark Smith had given them his approval - and in Manchester that counted a great deal. Any relationship they had ended when Smith and his girlfriend and band manager, Kay Caroll, purposely avoided meeting Hucknall and Moss one time, by stepping into a shop doorway as they passed in the city centre.

It all helped to strengthen the band's resolve, they thrived on rejection. They were booked into the Mayflower again and when only 30 people turned up they used it as a grand rehearsal. They played more than 50 songs, every song they knew, and did not leave the stage for two and a half hours. It was a reactionary stance typical of the band.

The band suddenly found inspiration at the other end of the M62 motorway in Liverpool. They were booked to appear at Eric's Club, a breeding ground for burgeoning New Wave talent like Echo and The Bunnymen, Wah! and The Teardrop Explodes. They arrived at the venue in a taxi carrying just a guitar, bass, microphone and a pair of drumsticks. There had been a mix-up over the hire of a van and Turner, just hours before they were due on stage, had persuaded a taxi-driver to take them through the snow to Liverpool for an agreed £20 fee. Hucknall had been on a polytechnic trip to London and travelled by train directly to Liverpool.

'We were sick of the 15 minute guitar solos...'

The band, or, more accurately, Hucknall, since he did all the talking, had no truck with the esoteric outlook of most of their peers. "We've got to try and get our songs across to people. We want them to hear our songs - it's like being a salesman, you've got to go out and say, 'Get a load of these songs', you've got to shove it down their throats, there's no sin in that," he said. He was already anticipating fame: "Fame's fine, but fame doesn't last unless you're producing something good."

Unwittingly, Hucknall had immediately and carelessly broken several taboos of the UK music press: he openly desired fame and recognised the need to market his songs properly ('salesman' was his word). Music journalists wanted to champion the diffident, the gawk, the suffered. They wanted art, not sales talk: people like Mick Hucknall could look after themselves without their help.

The Frantic Elevators had a manifesto of sorts and it was influenced by Hucknall's experiences at polytechnic. "It was just mad clothes and mad ideas - almost like applying Marxism to music. It was all about fucking the music business up. We were sick of the 15 minute guitar solos. We took the piss out of guitar solos. They're ridiculous, rambling fucking nonsense," said Hucknall.

STUFF THE SUPERSTARS
FUNHOUSE AT THE MAYFLOWER CLUB
SAT 28TH JULY   DOORS OPEN 1.30 p.m. BANDS FROM 2.00 TILL LATE.

IN ORDER OF APPEARANCE......

HAMSTERS   LUDUS
ELTI FITS   THE LIGGERS
ARMED FORCE   THE FALL
FRANTIC ELEVATORS   THE DISTRACTIONS
JOY DIVISION   JON THE POSTMAN
                        PSYCHEDELIC R'N'R 5 SKINNERS

TICKETS AVAILABLE FROM:- DISCOUNT RECORDS (Underground Market)
                         PICCADILLY RECORDS (Piccadilly Plaza)

TICKETS £1.50   TICKETS £1.50   TICKETS £1.50

STUFF THE SUPERSTARS SPECIAL FESTIVAL.....SATURDAY 28th JULY
FUNHOUSE AT THE MAYFLOWER CLUB.............
BAR 1.30 - 3.0, & 5.30 TILL LATE. FOOD AVAILABLE ALL DAY......
RECORDS, SHIRTS, FANZINES, etc, ON SALE (CHEAP!!!).........
ALL PROFITS AFTER EXPENSES WILL BE SPLIT EQUALLY BETWEEN THE BANDS.

BUSES:-
From Piccadilly: 125,126,160,
204,205,206,207,208,209,210,
211,212,213,234,235.
From Cheetham/Clayton: 53.
From Old Trafford/Moss Side:53.
From Gorton & Hyde 125,207-212
From Droylsden: 169, 170.
From Didsbury & Burnage:169,170

'They had this collection of very odd, very short songs that didn't seem to fit anywhere'.

The club was run by Roger Eagle, an R&B and soul archivist and veteran of the North West music scene. He had been behind the famous Manchester club, the Twisted Wheel, in the Sixties. He saw Hucknall dust the snow off his coat and walk straight to the stage and help set up the gear. "They were a gawky Manchester band who had no frills about them, just delivered really good music. But Mick had this amazing voice. They were out of time in the aftermath of punk. They had this collection of very odd, very short songs that didn't seem to fit anywhere," said Eagle. He was to become a crucial ally.

The sound of the band was changing discernibly, the choppy edge giving way to basic rhythm and blues arrangements. Eagle had a real affection for the group and was influencing their sound. He provided support spots at the club and funded the release of their next single 'You Know What You Told Me' b/w 'Production Prevention' on Eric's Records in December 1980. Eagle, and his business partner Pete Fulwell, had effectively become managers of the group while Richard Watt concentrated on a flourishing photography career. Eagle secured a regular Saturday spot at another popular Liverpool club called Adam's and the band became so synonymous with the city they were often billed as 'Liverpool's Finest'.

There was initially acrimony in the split from TJM. Davidson did not have the finance to put out a single himself but he did

not wish to see a band he had invested in move on to success with another label. He had hardly covered his costs and it would have meant his time and money was all but wasted. Stupidly, the band decided on direct and illegal action to resolve matters. They broke into his office to find their recording contract so that they could destroy it and claim it had never existed.

They could not find the contract but the issue was peaceably settled when Hucknall made a final plea to Davidson to release them. He agreed, on condition that they signed a letter stating that he maintained the rights to material recorded by The Frantic Elevators for his label and a 50/50 publishing split from any subsequent royalties from the songs.

'You Know What You Told Me' was an unusual song, Hucknall's voice almost drowning in a wash of whistles, tambourines and out-of-time drumming. He tried to bring a semblance of tune to the chaos but ultimately failed. 'Production Prevention' was a return to the stark, punky touch better executed by others. The rhythm section was, as ever, tied to simplicity but Moss indulged in some interesting hot-wired guitar meandering.

Seven months later, in the summer of 1981, after Eagle had himself run unavoidably into a financial crisis, the band released the much stronger single, 'Searching For The Only One' b/w 'Hunchback Of Notre Dame'. It was released on

Crackin' Up Records, another venture supported solely by Eagle's altruism and dwindling financial resources. The song was fresh, if clumsy, but for once the band introduced light and shade into their music. Compared with their first two records, it showed that there was talent at work within the band. John Peel again enthused; the music press, especially *Melody Maker*, gave it tacit approval; even a show at Manchester's Gallery Club was packed... the record failed to sell.

Rather ambitiously, Eagle recorded one of their shows with tentative plans for a live album. He believed the rawness, the voice, the energy and their very appeal lay within a live context. It was, chiefly because of the band's wishes, never released although Eagle, to this day, thinks the tape would have established The Frantic Elevators as a top-notch, slightly off-the-wall UK rhythm and blues outfit. The tape was later appropriated by Simply Red's management and kept from public consumption.

Eagle, as many others would do in the years to follow, had fallen in love with Hucknall's voice. He saw him as his protégé but he was too chivalrous to suggest what might have been obvious. A writer calling himself 'Whizzo' in *City Fun* was less tactful in a live review: 'And so on come The Frantic Elevators. Groan, splurt, what bores. Pathetic songs, pedestrian bass, plastic drummer and cherubim singer. The singer has actually got a good voice but the songs are so crap it's wasted.'

Manchester and Mick Hucknall were out of kilter; the network that had propelled other bands was a triffid entwined around his legs. He was treated with ridicule, or worse, indifference. There was not enough pose or attitude about The Frantic Elevators; they were solid but mundane, also-rans in fact.

He was in the wrong city at the wrong time. It was a while before he realised he was also in the wrong band. The Frantic Elevators had been a natural extension of the friendship between the members. Hucknall apart, they held only mild pretensions to pop stardom but their musicianship was limited and their song writing skills only frail. The distance between the Beatles-fired aspirations and their skeletal songs was huge.

Hucknall delved increasingly into black music. The first record he had bought was Diana Ross' 'Doobedood'ndoobe' on Tamla Motown in June 1972. The singers were more authentic. They had a richness and a subtlety; in it he saw his own musical calling. He spent many evenings in the company of Roger Eagle and his massive collection of soul and rhythm and blues records.

Hucknall did not believe the group was capturing the bluesy sound he could hear in his head. "We were playing, or trying to play, R&B, but, unfortunately, bless their hearts, the lads didn't have a clue. We'd been thrashing away making all this odd music, then I started to write things that were based around R&B chords and they couldn't really express it," he said.

There were several meetings between Hucknall and Moss and they considered replacing the rhythm section and possibly augmenting the line-up with a saxophone player. They were in flux but received a boost when they met Elliot Rashman, the entertainment's manager at Manchester Polytechnic who had booked the band on a recommendation from both Roger Eagle and his close friend, bassist Tony Bowers.

That show was the beginning of the rest of Hucknall's and Rashman's lives. Rashman, fast approaching 30, had willed the moment. He had taken to wearing a trilby and a long coat and had fallen in love with the notion of showbiz management. He just needed an artist. It was almost the epiphany as he saw Hucknall - earnest, captivating, young, and in command of a voice steeped in soul classicism - on the stage before him. "Mick blew my mind. I knew it was a special voice. I saw my life flash in front of me," said Rashman later.

The Dancing Dead

'Mick blew my mind. I knew it was a special voice. I saw my life flash in front of me'.

The new benefactor offered them the world, but began with more support spots at the polytechnic. It was the first time they had met someone so slick and experienced in the music business. On a daily basis, through his job at the polytechnic, he spoke to record companies, agents and managers and his book of contacts was heavy with names and numbers.

Rashman's enthusiasm was infectious but almost immediately he was drawn to Hucknall, to the exclusion of the rest of the group. He had a direct and focused manner that impressed the singer and within a few months Hucknall was a regular feature in Rashman's office. Their plans were still vague but they were being carefully nurtured all the same.

Before Rashman's arrival the band had decided to release a single on their own label. The National Westminster bank gave them a £1,000 loan and they recorded two songs, 'Holding Back The Years' and 'Pistols In My Brain'. They had enough money left to cover pressing and printing and also to record a potential second single, a track called 'Haven't Got The Power'.

Hucknall had written the basic structure of 'Holding Back The Years' in 1977; it was one of his first ever songs. "Most would have put out a more up-tempo thing, but that was the sort of band they were - flying in the face of fashion.

'It was an absolute disaster because we just thought people would be interested enough to buy it'.

I remember saying at the time, 'No one's going to fucking play that, why don't you put the other side out?'" said Neil Moss' brother, Ian.

The group collected the singles themselves from the pressing plant in London and left copies at the music press and Radio One while they were in the capital. Released in October 1982, it showed off their new penchant for sweet, soulful music with even a hint of Neil Young in the guitar work. Sadly, it also revealed their marketing ineptitude. Their 'label', No Waiting Records, was a farce and the only redeeming factor was the song itself, a marvellously mature ballad.

The sleeve, a close-up photograph of Hucknall, a gun in his hand with the barrel inserted into his mouth, illustrated the B-side track and was obviously incongruous to the main song. They forgot to include the band's name on the middle of the record and, most regrettably, there was no distribution or promotion. "We thought that releasing records was like doing gigs - you did it by osmosis! It went out into a void. It was an absolute disaster because we just thought people would be interested enough to buy it," said Turner. Hucknall placed the disc on the juke box of the Whitegates pub in the city centre and sang along with himself as he dreamed of better days.

The initial failure of 'Holding Back The Years' was a salutary lesson in the power of marketing. It would sell millions just four years later and top the American singles chart, but without backing it was ignored completely. In fact, someone around the band at the time remembered the sales figure to be 11 copies! Admittedly, The Frantic Elevators' version had more raw edges and was recorded on a much smaller budget, but the chords, melody and atmosphere were identical. It also had a fragile, apologetic quality that did not make the later version.

Two months after its release, in a pitiable attempt to infiltrate the Christmas market, the record was re-issued. This basically amounted to band members again telling friends that they had records to sell if they were interested. There was hardly a response and the records were left in boxes.

The fiasco meant that the band were crippled with debts and to compound the misery the flat Hucknall shared with Moss was burgled three times within the space of a few weeks. The infamous riots of 1981 had been particularly fierce just a half mile down the road in Moss Side and the tension of violence was unbearable. There was an aura around the group of sadness. The gods were against them and their last chance had slipped away.

Hucknall, incidentally, had managed to fund both himself and his contribution to the group entirely on income from his student grant and unemployment benefits. The benefit system in the UK at the time was quite liberal and provided enough sustenance for a dole culture to exist whereby aspiring musicians, actors and artists of all persuasions could survive without the threat of restart interviews, 'job-clubs' and other pressures designed to quash such a culture.

His single minded ambition meant that he would rather suffer hardship than compromise his commitment to music. Friends said he often mocked the idea of finding a 'proper job', he was well versed in surviving on a shoestring and manipulated the benefits system so that he could concentrate resolutely on music.

Ian Moss could sense Hucknall's frustration as The Frantic Elevators lumbered onwards but not upwards. "He was getting more and more dissatisfied. Although the direction had changed and they were getting more R&B based, he wanted to go the whole hog and felt the rest of them weren't cutting it. I remember Mick and Neil were going to sack the other two for quite a while," he said.

A rare bright spot during the band's final days was their success in securing Radio One sessions. In a seven month spell in 1981 they were booked to record three different sessions, the first for John Peel in February, the second for Richard Skinner in March and the final one for John Peel again in September. Although the band were unaware of the fact, the last session of five songs was effectively the parting snapshot of Frantic Elevators' material - 'And I Don't Care (Nobody Stays Here)', 'After Hanging Around', 'What To Do?', 'I'm Not To See Her' and 'Ice Cream And Wafers'.

One of their final concerts was at the Band On The Wall. Towards the end of the set Hucknall was preparing to sing a blues cover but Neil Moss said he was too drunk to play it. Afterwards Hucknall remonstrated with the guitarist and grumbled that he was getting tired of the band's lack of professionalism.

SIMPLY
RED

Despite the friction, the hardship, the knock-backs and disparate musical forces at play in the group, Neil Moss was dumb struck when Hucknall announced his departure: they had sworn allegiance to the end. Music had been their life and it was intertwined with their friendship. Moss later told friends he had been left facing more than £200 in rent arrears when Hucknall left their shared flat. "It came as a great shock to Neil. He went into a very dark depression basically. He locked himself in a dark room and drank lots of whisky and took a lot of drugs for about 12 months. They were more than just in a band together. Neil had put all his eggs in one basket with Mick and he saw it as total betrayal," said his brother.

It is impossible to underestimate the impact the decision had on Neil Moss. It negated most of the work he had put into the band slavishly during the preceding years. "I think Elliot was a huge factor. Mick said to me that Elliot had replaced Neil as such. Neil had bolstered everything Mick had done and when Elliot started to play that role Neil was superfluous. I still think Mick did the right thing. Neil had to sort things out for himself, I thought the band had gone as far as they were going to go," said Ian Moss. Neil Moss' first remark after Hucknall announced he was quitting was, 'You're doing something with Elliot, aren't you?' Hucknall nodded.

The band continued without Hucknall for a few months, shortening their name to The Frantics. Neil Moss took over on vocals but their only concert was at the Thompson Arms, across the road from Chorlton Street Bus Station in the city's red light area.

Moss all but finished with music after leaving the pub's stage. He eventually lifted himself from the languor and cut out completely the drugs and alcohol. He obtained a university degree in physics and busied himself becoming a black belt in ju-jitsu and competing in numerous chess tournaments.

He became reacquainted with Hucknall some years later and was invited to Simply Red's show at Manchester's G-Mex venue. The Moss brothers went together and met Reg Hucknall outside the concert hall wearing a Simply Red T-shirt and other tour regalia. "Reg said to our Neil: 'You can't blame Mick for what he did', and Neil said, 'Well, it's funny because when we used to be rehearsing at your house, you were always shouting up, 'Turn that bloody rubbish down!'" said Ian Moss.

Hucknall was determined to organise the rest of his career with the utmost application. He recorded several demo tapes with a view to a solo deal and sang briefly with a rhythm and blues group from Liverpool called The Lawnmower. He concentrated mainly on his own work, inviting musicians to accompany him on a session basis. He took singing advice from an actress friend and began to view himself as a singer rather than a band member who happened to sing.

The curse that had struck The Frantic Elevators overlooked Hucknall completely and he immediately received positive reactions to demo tapes. One of the first on the phone to Rashman (allegedly, since it has never been substantiated but was to form a large part of Hucknall's A&R mythology) was the powerful Seymour Stein, the head of Sire Records in the US. At the time, Hucknall was warming again to the notion of fronting a group. Stein wanted a solo performer. He soon found what he wanted, a dance diva called Madonna.

Warners, to whom, through a convoluted route, Hucknall eventually signed, offered a tentative deal but the finance was not enough to support a group. "I was half doing this deal with Warners, which in the end just collapsed. I was a singer on my

> ## 'Neil had put all his eggs in one basket with Mick and he saw it as total betrayal'.

own, without a band, which meant they could just say, 'Look, you haven't got anything. What have you got to offer us except a voice?'" he explained to *City Life*, a listings magazine which had started in Manchester in 1983.

A loose quartet consisting of Hucknall, David Rowbotham (guitar), Peter Hucker (bass) and Chris Joyce (drums) began playing together. Sometimes Tony Doyle from Lawnmower stood in on bass and for a short period a keyboard player, Kate Crabtree, also played with them. Rowbotham, Joyce and Tony Bowers had played together in a group called The Mothmen, with whom Rashman had risen from roadie to manager before they disbanded. It was noteworthy that Rashman generally looked to his friends from either the Didsbury clique, of which he was part, or the polytechnic to find musical partners for his new charge. He was, in typical music business style, finding jobs for the boys.

Kate Crabtree, from the West Yorkshire town of Todmorden, became involved with the line-up after playing with the reggae band Yore Next who had supported Southern Death Cult on a UK tour during 1983. A former pupil at Manchester School of Music, she was playing the rebel at the time - her hair was cut into a Mohican and dyed purple, she had fallen out with her parents and become a protégée of the eccentric producer Martin Hannett.

At first she was unsure about joining so Rashman travelled to Todmorden to speak to her and her parents. "He turned up in a raincoat. My dad didn't like him straight away. He started going on about how, if I joined the band, I would be mega famous. My dad told me not to believe a word he was saying. He was a sharp little Jewish man," she said.

Hucknall enjoyed working with Rowbotham, despite his rock leanings, and the pair appeared to form a promising song writing partnership. Rowbotham was also a friend of Martin

'It was so obvious to me that he was going to be successful'.

Hannett who had worked regularly at Stockport's salubrious Strawberry Studios. He was owed, in kind, some free studio time and after a meeting with Rashman he was cajoled into spending it with Hucknall and his colleagues. The deal was simple - if the demo tape secured the band a record contract Hannett would produce at least one of the band's forthcoming singles. Nothing, of course, was signed to this effect; Hannett usually worked on trust.

In July 1983 they recorded four songs over three nights when the studio was empty of paying customers. The songs were: 'Hell From You', 'All Through The Day', 'Take A Look' and 'Make Me Feel Good', the last of which was written, music and lyrics, by Rowbotham alone. According to Kate Crabtree, Hucknall's voice was nothing like the voice that later made it on to vinyl with Simply Red. She thought he sounded like Slade's Noddy Holder!

She also claims that many of Hucknall's biographical details from the era have been misrepresented. From the time Kate Crabtree joined in April 1983, each musician was told that Rashman was representing a band, not a solo singer, and that Rowbotham's role appeared to be almost on a par with Hucknall's. "Mick was dead friendly at first," she said. "He seemed unsure of his future. He did not seem to take much notice of Elliot, but then they began to pull away from the rest of the band."

Before then, Hucknall had mixed happily with the other musicians. Kate Crabtree was persuaded to leave her home town and move to Hulme to be based near them. After rehearsals Hucknall would walk into Rusholme with the others, hunting out his favourite kebabs. On one occasion, while Kate's parents were away, she held a four day party at their home in Todmorden. Hannet over-indulged and ripped the gas fire from a wall, and Hucknall disappeared into the attic for some time with a girl. The noise from the party was such that the police were called and a local magistrate also paid a visit.

Despite promises of a contract with Rashman, none of the musicians received one, even though he once told them: "Get your passports ready, we are all going to America." The mood changed drastically once Seymour Stein had contacted Rashman and suggested that Hucknall become a solo performer. Hucknall, constantly idolised by Rashman, became aloof and eventually announced to the band that they could either stay on as session players, or leave.

Kate Crabtree was upset because she felt she had been deceived. After speaking to Dave Rowbotham, she resolved to save her dignity and refused to accept a reduction in her role in the group. "We never did get to sign the contract that Elliot was always talking about and I never got a penny out of the group. It was all bullshit, we were all used as far as I can make out." After tours backing performers as varied as Shakin' Stevens, Haircut 100 and various reggae bands, Crabtree finished her professional career and in 1993 was living in Manchester's gangland area, Alexandra Park.

Martin Hannett did not get to work with Hucknall again and neither was his suggestion that the band be named Ghost Shirt taken up. "My main disgust is that they used Martin Hannett. He took care of me and was a very good producer but they just used him," said Kate. Hannett, a man prone to self-pity, depression, naïvety, strokes of genius and the misuse of medication, died in 1990, so a leading player in the evolution of Mick Hucknall was lost to memory. Hannett's good friend, Dave Rowbotham, also died soon afterwards. A heroin user, he had successfully completed a detoxification programme but was the victim of an axe attack and died in his home.

By Christmas 1983 it was clear that Rowbotham and Rashman could no longer work together, their personal lives having become linked in bizarre fashion. Rashman had split with his wife, Lyndsay, and she had begun to see Rowbotham. Some time later Rashman began a relationship with Rowbotham's regular girlfriend, Louise, and the guitarist was not happy to see the love-triangle develop into a quadrilaterial.

Andy Dodd (left) and Elliot Rashman, Simply Red's management team.

Rashman found a replacement guitarist from the neighbourhood in north Manchester where he had grown up. Dave Fryman was working as a schoolteacher, had celebrated his 30th birthday and had all but given up hope of becoming a full-time musician. In fact, he was more than happy teaching. Rashman coaxed, begged and pushed the reticent Fryman into working with Hucknall, whose talent he initially failed to see and whose manner he did not particularly like.

Eddie Sherwood, a drummer well known on the Manchester scene, also joined after listening to Rashman's impeccable sales talk and the line-up was completed by bassist Ian Morris, better known as Mog. He had previously played with The Smirks, a Manchester group labelled 'post punk pop' that had notched up three 'singles of the week' in *NME*. "I shared the same broad taste in music as Mick. We clicked immediately. I'd actually seen him in the Grant's Arms in Hulme some time before, playing pool. I was very impressed with him, his manner and the way he was dressed. He was a big-headed get, confident about what he was doing," said Mog.

Mog instantly knew where Hucknall's voice and drive would take the group and wanted to be part of it. He decided to curtail a promising acting career that had already secured him a 13-episode run in the Channel Four soap opera, *Brookside* with a £600 per week pay packet. "I realised then it was something that was going to be very famous and successful. Through talking to him what impressed me was his vision, it was so obvious to me that he was going to be successful," he said.

Mog was seasoned in the politics and subterfuge weaving through pop groups and saw, in his own words, that Hucknall and Rashman were 'in cahoots'. He naturally had to ask: "I was at Mick's birthday party and I was told that no matter what happened I would be in the band. I had asked about it because it was a worry. It was always stressed throughout that it was a band but there was a lot of double-speak going on. Mick and Elliot always said, 'It's a band, it's a band'. They used to talk about in four albums' time when Mick would do his solo album and I would go off to do some films," he said.

Mog later became an admirer of Rashman's business acumen but underneath the façade of professionalism, he saw a character he had witnessed around other bands. "He was as mouthy as he is now but, like with most bands, no one knew what the fuck was happening or what to do. I remember Dave Rowbotham used to call him 'Harry Paranoid, Top Rock Manager'. Elliot would put his fear and paranoia and his nervousness on top of everyone else. If there was nothing wrong, he'd still want to change it," he said.

A friend of Mog's, Keith Ojo, joined on trumpet and they all rehearsed twice a week. In between, Hucknall and Mog would work on material using acoustic guitars because, being unemployed, they had free time in the afternoons.

Hucknall's profile was high through hosting a regular club night at the polytechnic known as 'Black Rhythms'. Andy Spinoza, now a Manchester freelance journalist, was a regular on Wednesday nights. "It was a mainstay of my social scene. I chatted to him and I remember him making me up a tape. He was a well-established local figure. He was a character, you couldn't miss him. He announced himself with his red hair and his whole demeanour. He was the cool cat behind the decks. He was friendly enough but he knew he was it. Some would say it was arrogance but I would just say it was cool," said Spinoza.

Another polytechnic DJ, Joe Strong, shared a flat for a while with Hucknall and was also managed by Rashman. He fronted a group called Little Douglas but did not have the charisma of Hucknall. There was a period when Hucknall veered closely towards rockabilly. He had discovered Gene Vincent and leather jackets and Mog had received the nod partly because he owned a double bass.

The records played by Hucknall at the discos gave an indication of his later musical direction. The emphasis was on classic, traditional black soul music by the likes of James Brown, Otis Redding, Gladys Knight, Aretha Franklin and Marvin Gaye. Unlike many club DJs he did not necessarily spin the most obscure records; the tune and the rhythm were the only consideration, the soul snobs could go elsewhere.

Mog was having difficulty adapting to the hierarchical structure of the group. He was told that song writing credits and subsequent royalties would be Hucknall's. He accepted that Hucknall was chiefly devising the chords and vocal melodies but the whole group was involved in arrangements. He thought it unfair that one member should be due a greater amount when some of the others, himself and Fryman particularly, had devoted hundreds of hours to the project. "There was a confrontation between Elliot, Mick and me. They said I'd get an arranger's fee but I wanted more than that. The result of the confrontation was that I got fuck all," he said.

Surprisingly, despite the simmer of discontent, Hucknall and Mog became close and spent many nights together at clubs like The Hacienda and The Venue. The song writing issue was put aside as a business matter; it was a problem for Rashman and Mog, not Hucknall.

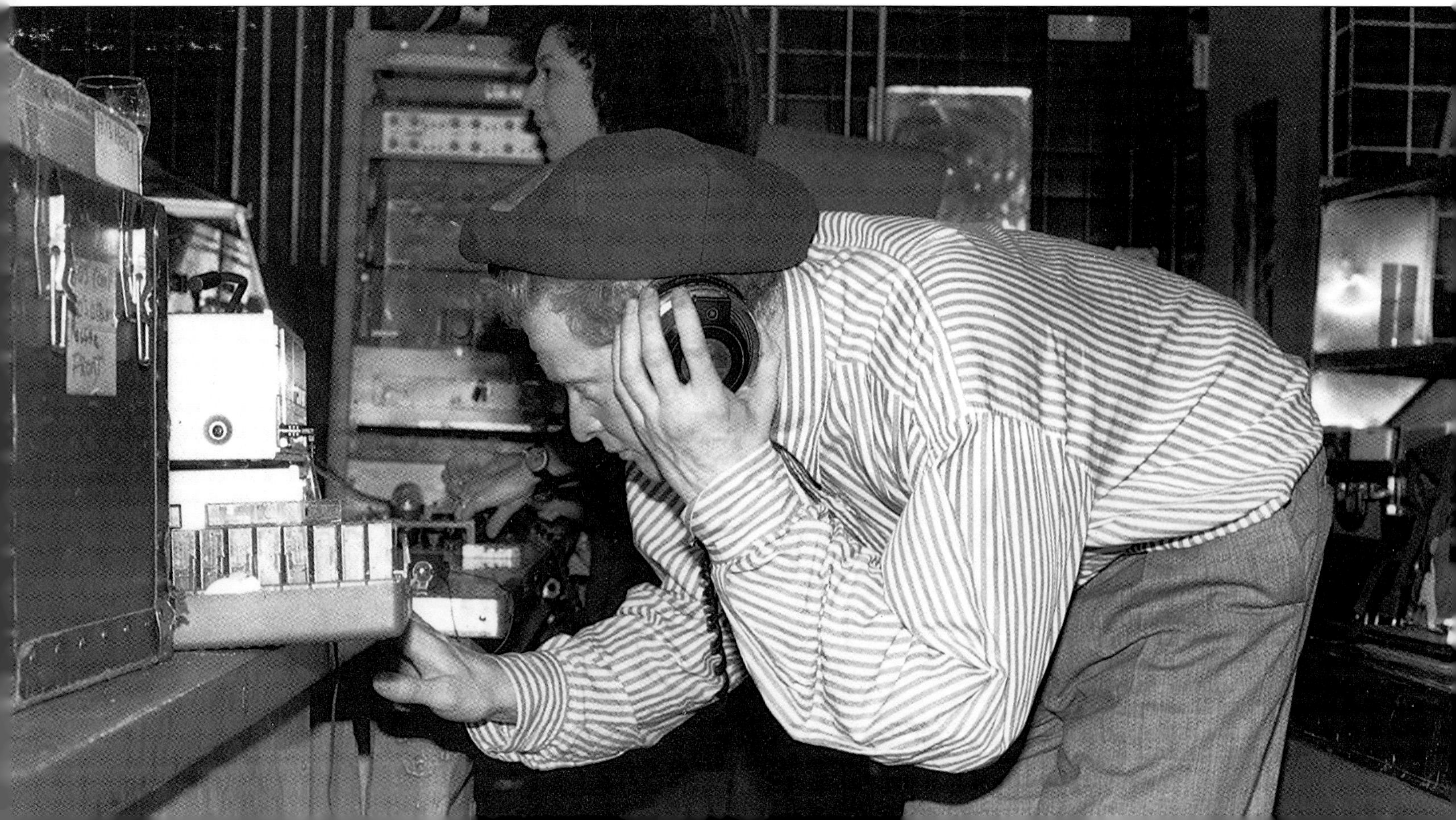

A poster designed by Hucknall to promote his discos.

The line-up had many changes of name and most of them centred around Hucknall. At different times during the early part of 1984 they were: Red and The Dancing Dead, Just Red, Red, World Service, All Red and Simply Red. Their first concert, under the name of World Service, was as support to Billy Bragg at the polytechnic in March 1984.

They evolved into a superb unit, blending wistful soul and hard funk with a late-night piano bar ambience, and by the summer of 1984 their shows in Manchester were alive with promise. In May they appeared at the Manhattan Sound club, an intimate, mainly gay venue, based amid the city's banks and insurance companies in Spring Gardens. A name had been settled upon, Simply Red. Hucknall had started to refer to himself as 'Red' because it crystallised his colouring, his favourite football team, Manchester United, and his politics.

On the day after the Manhattan Sound concert the name was being mentioned favourably by the same clique that had earlier rejected The Frantic Elevators. Simply Red were still not particularly cool or arty, but they were slick and earnest and had a sophistication of sorts.

After a show at the Band On The Wall Ojo left the group. The sound mix had not been favourable and, according to the other members, he had struggled to stay in time and tune. His fiery temper had already clashed with Hucknall's and the blend was flawed. Tony Bowers, who had earlier recorded some vaguely experimental music with Hucknall on his portastudio, played saxophone for a few months.

Rashman developed a dialogue with the A&R departments of several record companies but by July 1984 Hucknall was becoming frustrated with the delay in finding a deal. "It's important that we get something out, either on an independent or - I can't visualise it this soon - on a major," he told *City Life*. Mog also attended the interview, thought to be the first under the band's settled name, and the pair were photographed together.

City Life was a keen supporter of the band, especially one of its founders, Chris Paul. Along with other members of the magazine staff, he was a first point of contact for new groups.

'It was obvious immediately that Elliot was a complete believer in Mick...'

"It was obvious immediately that Elliot was a complete believer in Mick. They were both very confident about what they were doing. They didn't hustle anyone, but just let them know what was going on," he said.

Mog's initial impression of the bond between Rashman and Hucknall was accurate. "They lived together for a period. They used to sit up all night plotting. Elliot worshipped him. If Mick was to ever lose Elliot he'd be fucked, he'd have no stability at all," he said.

City Life agreed to co-promote a showcase concert, especially as Rashman would undertake most of the promotional work. The Tropicana, a sullied club in Oxford Road, was chosen as a venue. Chris Paul dealt closely with Rashman and had a taste of his management style. "It was very much built on favours and loyalty. He placed adverts with the magazine and wanted to build up a sort of trust between the people he was working with. He did not want anyone to disturb that balance," he said.

Mick Hucknall (left) sometime Red, ex-Frantic Elevators, now fronts World Service (aka Red and the Dancing Dead), writhed and screamed his way through a lively set in support of Alexei Sayle. They covered Talking Heads' 'Heaven', less ethereal than the original, with affected pauses — it was well received. They encored with 'Wounded Animal' and had the crowd writhing — along-a-Mick. If only Rob Graham had been there — World Service could've been the Next Big Thing. I suppose they might just make it without him.

A few weeks before the concert, Knaresborough-born trumpet player Tim Kellet joined the group. He was studying at the city's Royal Northern College of Music and had already guested with the neo-classical Manchester band Durutti Column. A Grade Eight player, he left his degree course part-way through to join the band. He was just 20 years old.

On Thursday November 1, 1984, on the same night that Sade appeared at the city's Apollo Theatre and New Model Army at The Hacienda, a posse of music business VIPs travelled to Manchester and took their place on the sticky dance floor next to the plastic palm trees in the club that had formerly been Tiffanys. "There must have been up to 500 people there. The atmosphere was electric and on the whole their performance fulfilled expectations. There was no denying Mick's presence, his charisma and, of course, his voice," said Spinoza.

Tony Michaelides, a DJ on Manchester's Piccadilly Radio and a respected record plugger, had arrived back from a trip to London on the evening of the concert. Simon Potts, the chief of Elektra UK and a friend of Michaelides, had arranged to stay with him and watch the Tropicana show. "I didn't want to go. I was knackered and just wanted to flop in an armchair." said Michaelides. "I'd not really heard of the band, they were not dishing tapes out ten a penny. I got there, there was me, Mr Manchester in inverted commas, and I realised I hardly knew anybody, it was all people who knew Simon. Record companies, being sheep, if Simon was after something, everyone was after it."

Mog looking up to Hucknall, but not for long.

The set was epitomised by the cover of Al Green's 'Love And Happiness'. It had been the first song they had learned and Hucknall wanted it as a reference point. They chose an eclectic set of covers, ranging from the *a capella* Taj Mahal track, 'Northern Lights', sung originally by Keith Ojo, to the Undertones' classic New Wave anthem 'Teenage Kicks'. They ran through Prince's '1999' in rehearsal but did not play it live. They were already playing 'Money's Too Tight (To Mention)' and a smoochy version of Talking Heads' 'Heaven'.

Their own songs, of which the set was three-quarters comprised, included tracks that would later make Simply Red's début album - 'Sad Old Red', 'Red Box', 'Picture Book', 'No Direction' and 'Holding Back The Years'. "Mick was a great performer. He didn't seem to be self-conscious at all. He would contort his face when he sang and was very lively. I remember they used to do a song called 'Wounded Animal' and he'd end up rolling around on the floor," said Chris Paul.

The review in *City Life* by Robert Graham was unintentionally heavy with irony: '...too often bands of this ilk (accomplished musicians with no image) languish a lifetime in pubs. Hopefully not this lot though.' Once the band had left the stage, Rashman ushered them into the dressing room and closed the door. The A&R men and anyone else on the guest list of 50 could sweat it out until the following morning.

A few days afterwards Simply Red appeared at the Leadmill club in Sheffield. The cracks were widening and tension had sprung within the group. The evening was long and laboured and several home-truths came home, especially to Mog. He wanted to wear a home-made waistcoat on stage but was challenged by Rashman. "Elliot said, 'You're not wearing that'. His manner with people was very bad a lot of the time. He could fuck people up. He could be conniving and manoeuvre things his way. It was not like, 'Are you sure about that Mog?' I told him to, 'Fuck off', it was a massive row... about a waistcoat."

Rashman was fastidious about the band's clothes. Inevitably, Hucknall's style was perfect and Rashman constantly told the others, "Look at Mick, I think he looks great but I'm really worried about the rest of you lads." He advised Mog to read back-issues of Vogue for fashion tips and took Fryman on a shopping trip. They returned with a grey jump-suit which Hucknall ridiculed.

On stage at Sheffield, Mog found his microphone stand had been moved towards the back. At previous concerts the band had adopted a straight line of three microphones at the front of the stage. "It was funny because for a while I was Elliot's favourite. He would say, 'You stole the show, jumping around and all that, it was great.' At the next rehearsal he was saying, 'We saw this reggae band the other night and the bassist was walking from side to side across the stage and then back again'. It was not choreography, they just wanted me at the back," said Mog. He was also told to remove a large CND sticker from his bass. The message, from Rashman: 'We'll never get into America with that on your guitar.'

Several A&R staff from Stiff Records attended the Sheffield show and called backstage afterwards. Rashman and Hucknall did the talking while the rest were told: 'Go to the bar or something'. In the event, Stiff promised to sign them but wanted them to nurture their sound for a year before releasing a début record. Hucknall and Rashman couldn't wait that long.

Unknown to most of the labels, Elektra UK was already ahead of the field by a considerable distance. Its parent American company, itself a division of Warner Bros, had opened a small office in London with just four staff whose brief was to basically act as an A&R department to find and develop new talent. Simon Potts, formerly of Arista Records, and his assistant, Saul Galpern, had seen Simply Red rehearse months before and already had a good relationship with Rashman and Hucknall. "There was a fondness. Rashman and Hucknall were fond of Simon and Saul. Whereas other people offered them more money, the band signed for the commitment rather than the advance," said Michaelides.

CBS offered the highest amount, reportedly an open cheque, signed but waiting for numbers to be filled in. The Elektra advance was £60,000, substantial enough to show a statement of intent without swamping them with unrealistic expectations. Crucially, Simply Red were to be the band used as a focus for the UK operation of the label. The promise was that they would be nurtured, encouraged and properly financed and, as the label's first signing, they would unquestionably be top priority. As a sign of ultimate trust in the group, Potts even agreed that they would not need to record demo tapes. They could go straight into the recording studio and put their music on to master tapes. It was a rare luxury.

'**Look at Mick, I think he looks great but I'm really worried about the rest of you lads**'.

The nature of the deal and the brilliant way it had been schemed was to form a fundamental part of Simply Red's ideology. It placed So What in the seat of power, to the exclusion of the musicians - present and future - in the group. Most managers secured their acts a record deal and then drew up a separate contract between themselves and their artist, but Rashman had put himself in the unusually strong position of finding his artist a solo deal in which he was officially included.

A new member joined Simply Red in the summer of 1984, Birmingham-born keyboard-player, Fritz McIntyre, another graduate of the Royal Northern College of Music and, in soul music vernacular, the son of a preacher man. He was 28-years-old and brought maturity and great accomplishment to the group. He had been playing semi-professionally in Manchester for a number of years.

There had been a running disagreement between Hucknall and Mog; the singer wanted a keyboard player and the bassist a full brass section. The pair had also disagreed about the band's sound. Mog wanted to maintain the raw touch ("We were both out of punk bands and I thought it was great having that energy with the soul singing") but Hucknall was keen to jettison it for a smoother, Americanised slant.

The line-up was far from finalised. Mog wanted to replace drummer Sherwood because he believed his timing was erratic. Hucknall wanted to give the drummer three warnings in the manner of a workplace, but Mog thought it would just delay the inevitable. The pair travelled to the Albert pub in Rusholme to give Sherwood the news. "I suppose I'm the man who invented sacking within Simply Red which isn't something that I'm proud of, but I just couldn't cope with Sherwood's time-keeping any more," said Mog. Sherwood, for his pains, had earlier been told he was 'a little gem' by Rashman.

Mog believed that, along with Hucknall and Fryman, he was part of a triangle of power within the musical base of Simply Red. When he did not receive any phone calls over Christmas 1984 from anyone connected with the band, intuition told him that his bags, although packed, were not marked for fame, kudos, wealth and travel with Simply Red. "There was suddenly a knock on the door. It was Mick, Dave and Elliot. I knew, I just knew. It was the bullet with my name on. They said I couldn't cut it in the recording studio. I was as angry as fuck. I kept saying, 'You're sacking me because I'm not a 'yes man'. The deal on the table was not the important thing. The upsetting thing was during that year I thought Mick had become a good friend. That was the upsetting thing, the betrayal. It was the loss of a friendship and them being dishonest," he said.

It was a move Hucknall was to repeat several times during his career. He was naturally reluctant to delve into the machinations of the decision. In simplistic terms, as related to anyone who inquired, people like Mog, Eddie Sherwood, and later Dave Fryman, were not good enough as musicians.

"I particularly like vocalists. The first time I heard Mick Hucknall's voice I thought it was the best white soul voice I'd ever heard and certainly the best new voice of the last 10 years," said Galpern. A decade later and Galpern was backing another glorious winner, Suede, signed, sealed and impeccably delivered by his own label, Nude Records. They also boasted a distinctive vocalist, Brett Anderson. The swagger was similar to Hucknall's if the influences and voice were not.

There was further discontent within Simply Red about the basis of the deal being struck. They learned that the band was not to sign to Elektra in the conventional sense of each member signing the contract. In fact, they would not need to sign anything at all. The structure of the deal was that a production company formed by Rashman and Hucknall, with Rashman's business partner Andy Dodd called So What Arts Ltd, would actually sign to Elektra. Under the agreement, So What would lease its acts, in effect just one group, Simply Red, to Elektra for the duration of the contract. When the musicians inquired they were told: 'Everyone does it like this these days'.

"I wasn't going to carry any dead weight. I gave them a thousand pounds each - what did they want? It's funny that those guys, when they were complaining about losing their places, never mentioned that they got that money. Our accountant went fucking bananas because we were living on borrowed money. I didn't have to do that and all I got was flack," Hucknall told *Q*.

Rashman, incidentally, later claimed Hucknall's remarks were misquoted by the magazine. An irate Mog called at the So What office threatening to, 'Throw either a table or Elliot through the window.' He was told the journalist had made a mistake, Hucknall had been misunderstood.

Further remarks by Hucknall provided little solace for

'I knew, I just knew. It was the bullet with my name on...'

Mog who, like Moss before him, slipped into a deep depression and a loss of confidence in both his playing and human nature. "Anybody who loses their job is going to be bitter. But it's their sadness not mine, they can't put their bad energy on me. They should get on with their own lives and not dwell on it because if they dwell on it, it's going to hurt them and they shouldn't hurt themselves like that," said Hucknall.

'I'd had enough of being on the dole, doing nothing and going nowhere...'

Rumours spread that Rashman was the Svengali, hiring and firing behind the Red façade. In an interview with *Muze*, a magazine covering the Manchester music scene, Hucknall manfully set the record straight: "Firstly, it wasn't Elliot, it was me. I sacked these people 'cos I make the decisions. These people didn't do it because they didn't make the grade. I don't mean that in a cruel way, but if they did make the grade what are they doing now? I'd had enough of being on the dole, doing nothing and going nowhere. And just being mates... I thought, 'Am I going to go for it this time? Yeah, I'm going for it - all the way.' All I'm gonna go for is the best. We were never really a steady band anyway. People were always joining or going. But the bitterness started when we signed the deal."

It was inevitable that the first line-up of Simply Red would feel acrimony. They had spent the best part of a year working on the material and while it was undoubtedly Hucknall's vision, their playing had shaped a sound that was to become Simply Red's own. Rehearsal tapes from the period showcase a band creating a tight, tuneful sound, admittedly focused on Hucknall's vocal gymnastics.

The musicians knew that there would be a great deal more to come than just £1,000. As the Elektra deal was finalised, they understandably felt as if they had been used and saw a project they had brought to fruition ripe for someone else to pick. Fryman, who actually remained a few months longer, and Mog were both respected as excellent and dedicated musicians. "If there is any justice in the world Elliot should get hold of some of the early tapes and release them. The band had a real edge and if Elliot did something like that it would enable the first line-up to get some money," said Chris Paul.

Hucknall's decision to sever himself from The Frantic Elevators had been the traumatic one (friends say he was distressed over Moss' reaction) and in comparison this was relatively easy: they were musicians with whom he had spent some time, not blood-brothers. Both Hucknall and Rashman also argued vehemently that it had always been a loose line-up without any promises or pretensions to be anything more than a backing group. Hadn't the rest noticed the name of the band? Or who was writing the chords and the melodies? Or who was at the front? Or who was making the decisions? Or who went to London to meet Elektra? Or who was shaping the group's image? Or how the contract was being drawn up?

Also, words like 'desperate' blurred in the circumstances with 'ambitious' and others, like 'cruel' and 'ruthless' were interchangeable with 'determined', 'single-minded' or 'focused'. While the terminology was ambiguous, Hucknall was merely adhering to an established route taken by all nascent stars - recognising that himself was now Himself.

The sacked musicians expected to be replaced by players of a very high calibre. When news filtered through that the new line-up was again drawn mainly from within Rashman's clique, it merely added to their disillusionment. The new rhythm section was the experienced Chris Joyce (drums) and Tony Bowers (bass), aged 27 and 32 respectively. Joyce, who had played on Hucknall's demo tapes, had earlier been dismissed by Mog and Hucknall for being 'too wooden'.

There was an amazing telephone conversation between Mog and his replacement. Bowers was living with the band's co-manager, Andy Dodd, and Mog wanted to chat with him about the decision. "Tony Bowers answered the phone and I told him what had happened, he said, 'Yes, I know'. It was all very Machiavellian," said Mog.

There was another irony. A few years earlier the comedy punk group, Alberto Y Los Trios Paranoias, had found their flagging career unexpectedly resurrected. They were invited to feature in an American television series and re-located to the US for a period. Their regular bassist, Tony Bowers, was replaced at the eleventh hour by... Mog.

The Elektra deal was completed in February 1985. Although Elektra UK had only a small staff, Potts and Galpern were given carte-blanche to single out the best people to work with the group. It was a professional, corporate unit with a rare personal touch.

Hucknall and Rashman had worked masterfully to turn around their woefully weak position of two years previously with The Frantic Elevators. Simply Red had everything The Frantic Elevators lacked - polished musicians (the sacked members would qualify this further by suggesting they were polished, *compliant* musicians), a strong image, professionalism, a defined musical style, finance, unsurpassed contacts and a proper record company. Rusty vans, rain and rejection already seemed a distant memory.

chapter 4

Colonel Parker and Elvis Presley; Brian Epstein and The Beatles; Peter Grant and Led Zeppelin; Ed Bicknell and Dire Straits; Paul McGuinness and U2: behind every successful artist is a brilliant manager willing to risk bankruptcy, divorce, heart attacks and psychosis on their behalf. The artist and the music becomes a crusade, the manager a ruthless zealot. And, when they are burned out and strung out, there are no thank-yous, more usually just the odd lawsuit or the occasional death threat. Pop management, like marriage or friendship, is beautiful until it ends.

Elliot Rashman and Mick Hucknall is a double act that has endured. Their two characters merge. They are both confident, single-minded, energetic, intelligent, aggressive. At the point where their characters merge lies the decision they both instinctively know to be right. They rarely disagree, and if they did, no one would get to hear.

The management-artist bond that holds them together is a shared vision. It has always been precise: they wanted to make Simply Red one of the most popular bands in the world. They have shaped the dream painstakingly, whether holed up in Hucknall's Hulme flat in 1983 or in a palatial hotel suite on the other side of the world a decade later. The rough plan had always been for Hucknall to record five classic albums, grow a beard, then retire to a Caribbean island and paint.

Rashman was brought up among Manchester's Jewish community in Higher Crumpsall and Cheetham Hill in north Manchester. There are palpable signs of the faith every 20 yards - a synagogue, a star of David on a school sign, shops selling bagels, men wearing skullcaps. There is also, lamentably, racist graffiti, daubed on the sides of warehouses along Cheetham Hill Road.

Shared Dreams

'They rarely disagree, and if they did, no one would get to hear'.

After leaving school Rashman studied at Manchester's Moston College of Further Education. He arrived at the college just as the Sixties was fizzling out but he had enough time to embrace the hippy culture. In his leather bolero he was a regular feature at The Magic Village, a tiny underground club in Manchester. He spoke to other regulars about his favourite West Coast bands like The Jefferson Airplane and The Grateful Dead, and sampled the various drugs on offer, especially hash. The club did not have a drinks licence but was open all night and people managed to remain energised.

James Morrison met Rashman through their mutual friend, Joe Seaberg, who died later of a drugs overdose. Morrison saw Rashman at The Magic Village and at the psychedelic discos held at the Jewish Lads' Brigade (J.L.B.) in Cheetham Hill. "I remember he fancied himself as a musician, and a bit of a troubadour. He once gave me this horrible acoustic guitar to do up for him."

Acid tabs were often dropped at The Magic Village and Morrison says he often saw Rashman there. "He smoked a fair bit of dope, but probably no more than anyone else at the time." Morrison was not particularly enamoured of Rashman's attitude. "He was aloof. He had an air of superciliousness about him. I don't think his condescension was backed by any intellectual standing. I've always thought he has the confidence of someone who's a bit ignorant, of having self-doubt," said Morrison.

Rashman later studied English Literature at Manchester Polytechnic but after attaining his degree could not find work. He had many friends in the affluent Didsbury area of Manchester and became manager of a group called The Mothmen comprised of former members of Albertos Y Los Trios Paranoias.

The group split and after a stint working as a joiner (apparently, he referred to his employment as 'carpentry') he found himself unemployed, supported by his teacher wife, Lyndsay. His break came when he learned through Michele Fryman, the wife of close friend Dave Fryman, that a job as entertainments' manager at UMIST (University of Manchester Institute of Science and Technology) was being advertised. He landed the job but soon moved to Manchester Polytechnic in the same position.

He was good at his job and kept his ears and mind open; bright but not too flash. His office was not the hangover recovery room of many student ents set-ups. He listened to the demo tapes and wanted to book happening bands. "He was much meeker and milder than he obviously is now as Mr, sort of, Top Line Management. I was working at Island Records at the time and he booked U2 in at the Poly. The gig was sold out and I came to him with a guest list of 102 people! He was worried about breaking the fire regulations and things like that, but I came on to him with the big record company bit and he got them all in," said Tony Michaelides.

Even then, though, Rashman was not a soft touch; far from it. He had the hard streak, the contemptuous put-down for the time-wasters and liggers. Mog remembers witnessing first-hand Rashman's gruffness. Ruby Turner was booked to play the polytechnic and arrived late with her backing band. After the show her manager collected the fee. Rashman was in his office with Mog and a few others. "Elliot chewed off this guy. He shouldn't have done it with all those people there, he was pretty nasty about it. Whether he did that to impress us or not I don't know. There was no need for it," he said.

Rashman ran the entertainment at the polytechnic with a firm hand and rarely showed a conciliatory air. "Elliot was horrendous, just totally ruthless," said Bob Venables, a member of the polytechnic's security staff. "He reckoned he had files on us all and could use them to sack us. He once had a meeting with all of us and said he had the dirt on each of us. It was a silly threat."

Venables was sacked after an altercation with Hucknall when he refused to help him carry his DJ equipment from the polytechnic's Didsbury site. Hucknall was angry and said there would be a reprisal. Venables travelled to the main site and when he arrived he was told he was no longer required to work his regular evening shift. "They said they were doing it because I was late and drunk on the job. I might have been on other nights but I wasn't that particular night. It was Mick who got me sacked, that's for definite," he said.

In his final six months at the polytechnic Rashman was clearly more interested in his outside activities and polytechnic staff saw that he was maximising the privileges of the job. One member of the security staff played keyboards occasionally with Hucknall and another, Reuben Hood, was taken on as a minder for Hucknall. The elevation of Hood did not surprise the others." He was Elliot's type of bloke," said Venables. "He believed in sticking by the rules. We couldn't let students in if they didn't have a pass. Sometimes they would forget them and we would let them in if we knew their faces, but not Reuben: he played it by the book."

Musicians traditionally gravitated to each other and formed friendships based on their creativity. It often meant non-players, like managers, were ostracised. Their relationship was limited because it could not transcend the rehearsal room,

'He's my best friend and he's like a brother. We look at each other and I know it's right'.

Dodd (seated) and Rashman.

recording studio, or the back of the van; the places where characters and ideas intermingled, where the sanctum of a group was built. Rashman and Hucknall were the exception to the rule.

"I'm so proud of what he's done. I've managed him for 11 years. His singing and song writing have grown, he's got older and more relaxed. He loves life, he's a music fanatic and doesn't waste time. He's my best friend and he's like a brother. We look at each other and I know it's right," Rashman told Q in 1991. It was not an over-statement.

Mark Cooper, a journalist writing chiefly for *Arena*, travelled to Milan in 1992 for a feature on Hucknall. After the formal interview he had dinner with the pair and had a rare insight. "Elliot Rashman adores him, unashamedly adores him, and that's the sort of key to their relationship really. He has seen him as a huge talent from Day One and is incredibly smitten by his artist, more than almost any manager I've met. I think the partnership is pretty much equal. I don't think anybody would tell Mick Hucknall what to do though," he said.

Colin Sinclair had met Rashman eight years earlier when Simply Red used rehearsal rooms based at his Boardwalk Club in Manchester city centre. "Some people are not too keen on him but I have always found him to be all right. He's one of those people who is very direct and some don't like that. He can be prickly at times but he gets exactly what he wants for his artist."

Simply Red finished using The Boardwalk for rehearsals after an argument about the use of a phone. The office door was locked and in petulance Hucknall kicked it open so that he could make a call. Rashman was contacted and his response was to send people to remove the band's equipment. "I suppose it shows the way that he deals with things, he made sure that nothing like that would happen again," said Sinclair.

When he first met Hucknall, Rashman was living in Didsbury and had embraced its culture of futons, whole food, media wannabe's, bedsits and musicians. He was driving around in a customised VW Beetle. He moved to the West Yorkshire town of Hebden Bridge where a similar stylistic life existed against the millstone grit of the Pennines. Along with many other in-comers he had discovered a form of Bohemian nirvana just 25 miles out of Manchester. He bought a small stone cottage and before water was installed he mounted two huge speakers on the walls and carefully assembled his huge record collection. Like Hucknall, he was a fan, and that was important to them both.

The country retreat became a feature of their weekends. Other friends were invited to share a spliff and the country air with them. It was a pleasure to share Rashman's company. Always, even when he was light-headed at the end of the evening, he would ask questions, eager to learn, proud to manage Mick Hucknall, anxious for success. It was peculiar that although his ambition was palpable, it was broadcast in a laidback, joss-stick flavoured environment. Rashman was part-hippy, part-capitalist; pop music had been driven since the mid-Sixties by people of the same persuasion.

Hucknall summarised their approach when he told an interviewer: "We use the industry and ride it and we're kind and polite to people who are kind and polite to us. It is a business, and you better get used to it quickly or it'll use you. But you don't have to be a pig." An insider referred to their deliberated style as, 'almost scientific'.

Although hardly known, Rashman is actually the co-manager of Simply Red, the other manager is Andy Dodd. While Rashman effectively fronts the group, Dodd deals with administrative matters. "When Elliot upsets people, Andy goes in afterwards and smoothes everything out!" explained a music business colleague. The pair run So What with a small staff in run-down quarters in the centre of Manchester, the name of their company taken from the famous Miles Davis' track.

The first recording by the new Simply Red aggregate was in Amsterdam in March 1985. Elektra pulled off a coup when the experienced American producer Stewart Levine agreed to produce the band. He had worked with black legends like B.B. King, Womack and Womack, Randy Crawford and The Crusaders but was tired of the formula and relished a group that was youthful, raw (malleable perhaps?), predominantly white and preferably English. He did not receive a work permit from the British government in time and they had to record in Holland where two songs went on to tape - 'Money's Too Tight (To Mention)' and 'Open Up The Red Box'.

Three years earlier, when Hucknall was a regular at Sandpiper's Soul Club in Manchester, he heard the track 'Money's Too Tight (To Mention)' by an American group called The Valentine Brothers. He had played it himself at his Black Rhythms disco. It had been a dance floor hit but since it was largely overlooked by radio DJs, it only reached number 73 in the UK charts. Apart from the song's soulfulness, Hucknall was attracted to the lyrics. Although strewn with Americanisms like references to 'Reaganonics' ('Did the earth move for you Nancy?'), dollar bills and Congress, the song was an authentic slice of ghetto poetry with the timeless refrain of a shortage of money.

Simply Red's version was released as a single in June 1985. It stayed close to the original and its seductive tones picked up heavy radio play. MTV, which ignored the Valentines' version, began broadcasting theirs in heavy rotation. Cynics would argue that this was a vignette of the rest of Simply Red's career.

The video was part of the image-branding to evolve out of Hucknall's natural style at the time. Shot in a seedy bar, the

'When Elliot upsets people, Andy goes in afterwards and smoothes everything out!'

mood was an odd pitch between Dickensian ragamuffin and Thirties Chicago. It was suitably mundane to reflect the song's theme and was fairly distinctive, although the fizzy UK band, Jo Boxers, had been in the same bar, played the same pool table and wore the same flat caps and braces on an earlier occasion.

Tony Michaelides was the first to receive a white label and played it regularly on his late-night radio programme which was generally reserved for more left-field music. He was, after all, on a small fee from Elektra to 'vibe up interest' in Simply Red.

Hucknall was invited to the station to do an interview, thought to be his first ever on radio to promote Simply Red. "He was slightly nervous. He was a lot quieter then. He did not really have anything to shout his mouth off about. He was okay, I think Elliot came in with him," said Michaelides.

The single was the perfect introduction to the group's sound - classy, tuneful, easy-on-the-ear, vaguely political, confident, and there was enough room within the mix for Hucknall to show off his expansive vocal range. It peaked at number 13 in the national chart and stayed in the Top 40 for seven weeks, a healthy performance for a new group.

Dave Fryman discovered, in pathetic fashion, that he was not required for the forthcoming album. The tortuous wind-up to his departure had begun as he waited to board the plane to Holland. Hucknall told him that Simon Potts wanted him out and that quite possibly there was another guitarist waiting in Amsterdam ready to play on the record. Fryman, since he was in the departure lounge, made the journey. There was, in fact, no replacement guitarist but he heard Levine talking to Potts on the telephone about finding someone else.

Fryman could not take it all in: Rashman, a long-standing friend (they had been on holiday together with their wives), had persuaded him to leave a flourishing teaching career just a few weeks earlier but there was now a sudden urgency for him to leave.

Over the space of a few days his confidence was systematically destroyed. He was told he was too short (he bought suède boots with a two-inch high heel); too 'straight' (he bought a leather jacket); his glasses were 'not right' (he

single. They opened at Goldsmith's College in New Cross, London, on May 17 with tickets priced at £2 each. Roger Eagle booked them into The International in Manchester on June 17. Rashman appeared to be developing paranoiac tendencies first noticed by Rowbotham. He was forever around the band, protecting and cajoling, and generally looking after His Boys with a painful intensity. He was, though unlikely to admit it, learning his trade and over-zealousness was a natural side-effect of the process.

Michaelides did some exemplary hustling and persuaded Piccadilly Radio to tape the Manchester show for later broadcast. The concert, Richardson's début, on June 15 was taped but Hucknall and Rashman were not happy with the sound mix and refused to allow it to be broadcast.

'You go from being nobody and no one really cares what you say to a situation where people hang on your every word'.

bought contact lenses but they made his eyes sore); his playing contained too much 'wallying' (he cut down on the solos). The final indignity was when he arrived home and discovered that his wife, Michele, had been told by Rashman before he even left for Holland that he was to be sacked. His marriage, like his involvement with Simply Red, ended soon afterwards.

His place was taken by the 20-year-old, former pupil at Manchester School of Music, Sylvan Richardson. Although classically-trained, Richardson had been spotted in a jazz combo called Inheritance. Andy Dodd had booked them for a jazz festival in Bradford when he worked for Jazz North West and had made a note of his name.

He was given a two-week trial and rehearsed solidly with the group. He was struck - amazed even - by the level of professionalism; it was inspiring rather than intimidating. "The first impressions were good, they were friendly people. Mick has got quite an aura about him and I was aware of it immediately," he said.

Chris Paul fell foul of Rashman when he ran a gossip piece in *City Life* revealing that Chris Joyce had been taking drum lessons, which was not in itself unusual or a slur. Rashman, however, considered it an act of betrayal. He believed, not completely inaccurately, that Paul was making a point on behalf of the sacked musicians, some of whom were his friends. There was retribution for his perfidy - Elektra Records ceased to advertise Simply Red's records in the magazine.

A handful of shows were organised around the release of the

Hucknall had been ignored for years; they were now clamouring for his attention. He had precious little experience of slim, inconspicuous tape recorders placed just a few inches away from his mouth. "They were very enjoyable times but also very pressured times for me personally. There I was, an urchin basically, who'd been on the dole for four years. I'd got this band together and the first single I release is a hit and immediately there's people doing interviews with me and this kind of stuff. You go from being nobody and no one really cares what you say to a situation where people hang on your every word," he said in a radio interview in December 1992.

Despite the bluster, both Hucknall and Rashman were extremely naïve; neither had been on pop's escalator before and as they alighted at each level they were sometimes caught blinded by the spotlight. Hucknall was frank, often too frank for most journalists. He was not aware that tiny fragments of conversation could rise serpent-like from a tape spool and spit back at him.

He had, almost regrettably, a view on everything and was quite charmless with it. "The greeting on the London scene is to fucking kiss each other! Darling! If someone kissed me like that I'd fucking hit 'em," he told *Time Out*.

jazz festival held over four nights in Hertfordshire early in July 1985. On a similar theme, they chose Ronnie Scott's famous club in Soho, London, as the venue for a major showcase concert on July 7.

The show at Ronnie Scott's was a resounding success. More than 400 people squeezed into the venue and the music press acclaimed the show. Pete Picton of *Sounds* wrote as if he had been privy to Hucknall's biographical fabric: 'It's a mixture of vintage black music brewed in Detroit and a hint of casual funk. The sort of nuggets you'd expect to find tastefully hidden in second hand record shops rather than blaring from speakers in gaudy discos.'

Early in August 1985 Simply Red headlined a festival in Manchester to promote International Youth Year. There were eight other bands on the bill, including James, but there was more than a hit single to set Simply Red apart. The group's entourage arrived with their own conspicuous security staff, additional speakers and far too many rock fineries than were required at a relatively low-key event. It was an unnecessary and ostentatious show of strength.

They received the first of thousands of magazine front covers in the July/August issue of *Muze*. Hucknall, in shades and a green top, was pictured hugging himself for all of Manchester to see. The same issue carried a review of a début single by another Manchester band later to become phenomenally successful, The Stone Roses.

Muze's editor, Mick Middles, met Hucknall in September 1985 when he was commissioned to write an article on the band for *Jamming!* magazine. It was an interesting joust. Hucknall had a self-satisfied sneer, he had once pestered Middles to write features on The Frantic Elevators. "Who are you then? Oh it's you is it... I knew you would come round to my way of thinking," gloated Hucknall. "I'll tell you something, this band is going to be massive, massive on a worldwide scale. I know this..." he continued.

In sales terms it appeared as if 'Money's Too Tight (To Mention)' was an early peak that they could not match. Their next three singles, 'Come To My Aid', 'Holding Back The Years' and 'Jericho' registered disappointing UK chart positions with 'Holding Back The Years' performing marginally better by reaching number 51. In Europe all three follow-up singles were hits and they did particularly well in Italy and Holland, but it was to be over a year before they were next in the upper reaches of the UK singles chart.

'Come To My Aid', co-written by Hucknall and McIntyre and the opening track from the forthcoming album, was released as a single in August 1985. There was another cover version as the extra track on the 12 inch - a rendition of Bill Withers' 'Granma's Hands'. The main track had a similar glossed sound as the first single but was watery and without a memorable chorus. The subject matter was again a note from the

'Who the hell do you think you are? Do it yourself you little prat'.

Backing Hucknall (Clockwise from top left) Chris Joyce, Tony Bowers, Fritz McIntyre, Tim Kellett.

'Money's Too Tight (To Mention)' gave rise to two issues that would hang like a Manchester rain cloud over Hucknall for most of his career: that he plagiarised black music and relied too heavily on cover versions. "It's largely because I'm white, and theoretically I'm involved in a black man's musical form. Because of the mostly middle-classness within the music media, they see that as some sort of cardinal sin," he said. He would later have to say infinitely more on the subject; the tone of defiance and hurt would not alter.

The Valentine Brothers, doubtlessly cheered to see their lament to poverty drawing in the cash, had no qualms about a white man re-inventing their music. "The first thing we asked the Valentines was, 'Did you get the money?' I had a horror that it would be going to some record company boss who bought it off them for $50. They did get it, and they were jubilant. They saw our hit as their hit and we got on like a house on fire," said Hucknall.

Elektra's vantage meant that Hucknall was soon fulfilling dreams. Simply Red opened for James Brown at some shows on his UK tour in May 1985, though the interaction between both bands was minimal. Simply Red were keen to establish themselves as an authentic musical group and appeared at a

The Simply Red line-up which recorded 'Picture Book'.

underclass but there was no melodic spark. Hucknall disagreed, even claiming the track was superior to their début.

Radio One did not playlist the record; news filtered through to Elektra that the programmers thought it was too slow for daytime radio. The music press had sharpened pencils. *NME* dismissed the single as 'Hokum!' and referred to the band as 'Simply Dreadful' while *Sounds* questioned why praise had been 'heaped like dung' upon their shoulders.

There was also the first rumblings of a clear media dislike for Hucknall and a manner considered to be arrogant. Under a small headline of, 'Hucknall A Prat Shock!' an *NME* gossip piece revealed that Hucknall had left his gloves behind in a taxi and clicked his fingers at WEA's press officer, Moira Bellos, to retrieve them. "Who the hell do you think you are? Do it yourself you little prat," was the alleged retort.

Elektra was true to its word and, initially at least, highly supportive of the band. The thrust of its promotion was Hucknall's distinctive features. His heart-shaped face framed by straggly golden tresses under a flat cap stared out wistfully from half-page adverts in the music press and posters in most UK cities. The other members of the band were surprised to see the emphasis so firmly on Hucknall - Rashman had previously told them Simply Red were a group. They were told that it was easier to promote one face rather than six. The view was accepted although they suspected the issue was not quite so simplistic.

The image of Hucknall was an obvious choice for the cover of Simply Red's début album, 'Picture Book'. The pastel colours were applied afterwards and gave the image extra warmth. The picture silently asserted that this was easy and assured music, perhaps sounding better after dark.

After the album's blurred opening with 'Come To My Aid', the band slipped into a jazz pastiche, 'Sad Old Red'. Hucknall was clearly recalling his home city as he sang of a place that did not have streets but 'just pure concrete'. From the bass running

adroitly through the scales to the slightly off-key piano doodling, this was a homage to the jazz cliché. 'Look At You Now' was an over-pristine modern funk track with much showy playing and not enough direction.

The re-invention of Talking Heads' 'Heaven' was imaginative and showed impeccable taste. It dated back to when Hucknall was working on material with Mog and they would sit in his flat picking out the chords on an acoustic guitar. The band removed the echoing translucence of the David Byrne/Jerry Harrison song and sat the track down by the piano and let the chords breathe for themselves. 'Jericho', in contrast, was too wordy and laboured and closed the first side as it had opened, out of focus.

The healthy heart of 'Picture Book' lay in the first two tracks on the B-side, 'Money's Too Tight (To Mention)' and 'Holding Back The Years'. Both songs indicated a rare depth for such young players. 'Open Up The Red Box' and the appropriately-titled 'No Direction', splashed around hopefully without actually arriving. The final title-track was a welcome flurry of experiment. Tony Bowers' bass was turned up in the mix and ran tightly alongside the drums in a reggae dub style. It was a glimpse of the band in relaxed mood, letting the atmosphere rule rather than fixing it to a standard pop formula.

'Picture Book' was undeniably patchy but it established Simply Red's musical trademarks. It was extremely slick but the voice riding through octaves with ease meant that blandness was largely avoided. In short, the song writing needed tightening but the components were present and augured well. Critical acclaim was unforthcoming but the public bought the record in reasonable quantities, hoisting it to number 34 in the UK charts in October 1985.

The album had been recorded at RAK Studios in London in a few short weeks and for the studious Richardson, pleased to be in a total musical environment, it represented the apex of his involvement with the group. "Mick was easy to work with in the studio because he knew what he wanted. Everything was very much cut and dried. I was creating stuff on the spot and it was only later on that I began to get hemmed in and musically frustrated," he said.

Most of the material had its antecedence from the previous 18 months but Richardson was soon privy to Hucknall's song writing technique. "We were basically set up in a large semi-circle. When he introduced a new song he would sit in the middle with his guitar. Everyone would pick up on what he was doing and it would evolve into a piece of music. He sang and played structures but we played around it," he said.

The coterie of people that had attended Simply Red's edgy formative shows were disappointed with the seamless feel of the record. It did not have the fire they associated with Hucknall; he was soon in partial agreement. In one interview he said it was bland and added: "A month after finishing it we were starting to see the faults. It had a gossamer sheen on it, like there was something in the way."

The group had been intimidated by Levine: he was a seasoned producer, they were nervous débutantes. "We had just started out and here was this guy who had produced Randy Crawford and The Crusaders and you think, 'He knows'. We didn't argue because we didn't know what we wanted anyway," said Hucknall. Levine had certainly erased too many rough edges but such an approach had hitherto been his production trademark; perhaps he was later vindicated by 'Picture Book's' incredible success when it sold steadily through the years.

Still, Hucknall felt the record captured a mood of freshness and could live with its flaws. "It sounded very new when it came out because it didn't really sound like anything else you've heard before. I listen to it now and parts of it remind me of Hulme and Moss Side - I think that's great because that's where I was at that time," said Hucknall in 1992.

The sacked musicians, Fryman and Mog especially, were peeved when they heard it. They expected that it would include some material they had helped initiate but they were taken aback to find so many reminders of their involvement. Dave Fryman at least had the scant compensation of receiving a co-writing credit for the track 'Open Up The Red Box'. "I was pretty pissed off when I heard 'Picture Book'. I thought of legal action, but it was very difficult," said Mog.

Considering the album's strong profile, the initial failure of 'Holding Back The Years' was a mystery. Elektra took out extensive advertising and utilised several promotional ploys including a limited edition gatefold seven-inch sleeve, free poster, and 'previously unreleased' tracks on the extended 12-inch. It was released in November 1985 and the Simply Red camp believed the ballad would be a Christmas hit. They had to settle for an ignominious number 51 but the issue was not over. There was also a flop across the Atlantic where 'Money's Too Tight (To Mention)' scraped into the bottom end of the *Billboard* Top 100.

As 1985 drew to a close there were industry rumours about the future of Elektra UK. The formation of the label and its marketing had been exemplary, but, seemingly, the American company was not satisfied. "They were blowing hot and cold. I heard that one minute they were on the phone enthusing about Simply Red and then they were moaning about something. I mean, to go Top 20 with your first single is brilliant. There was no logic for them to suddenly pull the plug," said Michaelides.

'They made life hell for Elliot, you just have no idea how intense it all was'.

Elektra UK was wound up and Simply Red's contract was passed on to WEA Records in the UK, another sub-division of the gigantic Warner Bros/Time-Warner conglomerate. There were fears that as an act discovered and nurtured by another label, Simply Red would not receive the same commitment. They were now one of a large number of acts scurrying for priority within the company. Rashman was especially worried, his name meant little to WEA's higher echelons and, like every other major label, they did not want a relative novice running the show. They wanted someone versed in the art of global rock management: Rashman eventually arrived at such a point.

Record companies worked insidiously; there was invariably a secret agenda. WEA harried and pushed Rashman, hoping he would consider handing over the group to a larger, established management company. "They made life hell for Elliot, you just have no idea how intense it all was," said Brian Turner, the former Frantic Elevator who remained a close friend.

After a handful of dates supporting UB40, Simply Red toured in their own right during November 1985. They played universities and polytechnics, except in Manchester where they performed at the cavernous Free Trade Hall, more often the home of the famous Hallé Orchestra.

WEA ushered in 1986 by releasing a new version of the mediocre 'Jericho' as a single. Unsurprisingly, the long, meandering verses, oblique chorus and preaching lyrical tone ('Listen boy, I'll tell you a thing') failed to entice the interest of DJs and the public. It missed the coveted Top 40 by 12 places.

Simply Red embarked on their first US tour in the spring of 1986, facing a marathon 40 dates. There was still a reluctance to accept that 'Holding Back The Years' had reached its rightful chart position. In May 1986 it was re-issued again, the third time the record had been released (or fourth if the Frantic Elevators' cosmetic 're-release' was included).

On May 17 it entered the chart at number 55, the group's fan base had taken it there. The next seven days were crucial; the record had to cross over to a more popular appeal and move up the charts. A fourth flop would have been disastrous, WEA had made a weighty financial investment and hits were required desperately. There was delight and relief when news filtered through that it had moved up to number 19. It climbed the chart steadily and eventually made number two for two weeks, held from the top by Dr and The Medics' cover version of Norman Greenbaum's 1970 hit 'Spirit in the Sky'.

In the US the single did even better and in July 1986 the previously unheard of British group made the top spot in the *Billboard* 100 for one week. Sales of 'Picture Book' were regenerated and it moved upwards and reached number two in the UK. At the end of 1986 it would be the 20th best-selling LP of the year. In a competitive US market place the album reached a creditable number 16.

While WEA and Simply Red were happy to see 'Holding Back The Years' receive the acclaim and sales it deserved, Neil Moss was about to find his life improve dramatically. As a co-writer credited with writing half of the music on the song, he was entitled to a quarter of the royalties. Due to the extensive international radio and television plays, Moss' amount was assessed at approximately £50,000 by 1990.

Hucknall revealed in January 1992 that Moss had not actually co-written the song. In an interview with *The Sunday Times* he said that he had written it by himself. "He [Moss] didn't actually write a note. That was a gesture to him for the three or four years we did write songs together," he said. Ian Moss, the brother of Neil Moss, confirmed that Hucknall's comments were true, so it was clear evidence of magnanimity by Hucknall.

Hucknall still frequented nightclubs, especially the Hacienda in Manchester. He began carrying an ornate walking stick with a cape slung over his shoulders. He saw it as sartorial elegance. "I saw the stick in a small shop in Scotland and for no other reason apart from the fact that I liked it, I bought the stick. And that was it, I fell in love with it," he explained.

Most Mancunians saw it as a pretentious statement. "I remember Mick as a gawky kid with a fat face, ginger hair and his mouth always open - I can't believe he is a major pop star," Martin Jackson, the former drummer with Swing Out Sister, told a reporter from the *Daily Star*. "Mick isn't very popular in Manchester now because he went and posed with a cape on and that bloody cane. People up here are too blunt for all that," he added. The bitchiness had started.

The bewildering promotional campaign for 'Holding Back The Years' meant there was no time for the band to visit the studio. In the absence of new material, WEA ill-advisedly released 'Open Up The Red Box' in July 1986; it meant that only one track from the album, 'Sad Old Red', had not been released as either an A-side, B-side or additional track on a single. Even by modern standards it was an unusual level of saturation.

It was a weak single and did not dent even the Top 60. It lost much of the momentum galvanised by 'Holding Back The Years'. In the US 'Money's Too Tight (To Mention)' was re-released to capitalise on their number one hit but it stalled at number 28. In the summer of 1986 Madonna was at the top with 'Papa Don't Preach', and her album 'True Blue' was shifting millions. In the Red corner, there was a quandary: did they now have a two-hit wonder on their hands?

'Mick isn't very popular in Manchester now because he went and posed with a cape on and that bloody cane'.

chapter 5

Pop, like sex and bingo and diet plans, sells newspapers. Two hit singles was enough to grant Mick Hucknall an audience with the new breed of young, slick hacks that frequented after-show parties and nightclubs. Readers of *The Sun* were told that Hucknall lived in a one-bedroom ground-floor flat in Manchester; he did not have a girlfriend (partly due to work); he enjoyed cooking Chinese and Indian food; he drank white wine and Guinness and he enjoyed cycling. Unlike most pop figures, he could turn in a good quote. "Britain gets what it deserves - and that means Su Pollard, Samantha Fox and 'The Chicken Song'," he told the *News Of The World*.

Taking The Tabloids

The press saw the anomaly: Hucknall's music was smooth and handsome and suggested sophistication, but he was from Manchester and his features were not dark and chiselled. It didn't add up.

He was drinking heavily, during 1986 he drank a bottle of wine each day. The tongue was loose and the candour remarkable. The media thrived off caricature and in August 1986 Hucknall inadvertently formed his own.

The *NME*'s Alan Jackson accompanied Simply Red on part of their American tour. The resulting piece, presented under the headline 'Sweet Surrender', inflicted serious damage to Hucknall's musical credibility. It presented to the world Hucknall as the chancer and the fornicator. He even missed the tour bus because of his after-show antics with a masseuse on a water bed! "He gets terribly irritable if he isn't getting it every day - ask anyone," said a helpful crew member. Hucknall flirted with a girl driving past in a sports car and was invited into the vehicle. "You've got to go with these situations, Alan," he told the hapless reporter.

'He gets terribly irritable if he isn't getting it every day - ask anyone'.

Jackson had caught Hucknall in a flashlight of surrealism. 'Holding Back The Years' had just left the country's number one spot and Hucknall's bizarre appearance, by conservative middle-American standards at least, looked set to plant itself firmly into their psyche. He was recognised everywhere, a restaurant owner in Minneapolis even refused money for a meal, saying the music was payment enough. Hucknall's behaviour, in truth, was no more extraordinary than the situation in which he suddenly found himself.

'I could never use a condom. I've never met a man who would...'

Though the union was doomed to be much-mythologised, girls and Mick Hucknall were already synonymous. A relatively stable relationship with the former girlfriend of Rashman's brother-in-law had fizzled out and Hucknall was a free spirit, making the most of opportunities. Even before the group's success he was remembered by Mog as 'a bit of a shagger'.

There was a world of difference between Mog's warm description of Hucknall's antics and the lascivious creature unleashed by Jackson. "It made me out to be like some carnal fucking beast, going around shagging everything I could get my hands on, like a dog with two dicks," Hucknall told *Melody Maker*.

It was safe to assume that Hucknall's sexual liaisons from this period were not encumbered by the use of a condom. It was before the apocalyptic AIDs warnings of 1987 and the condom was still seen as a form of contraception rather than a life-saver. "I could never use a condom. I've never met a man who would. They're horrible, they take the pleasure out of sex. It becomes like cattle. I'd imagine I was a bull if I was doing that, it's like you're being stopped from breeding. And I don't like girls being on the pill. It worries me what they're doing to themselves," he said.

An on-the-road clique formed around Hucknall, Joyce and Bowers. They were usually in each other's company although Hucknall began a close friendship with Kellet. "I don't really know how close anyone really is to Mick or how close he allows them to get. Before the band even formed it was masterminded, the whole thing was masterminded by Elliot and Mick. I think it is quite amazing what they are doing and I admire them for it. They are fulfilling their own prophecy," said Richardson.

In the US the band received a Grammy nomination as best new act of 1986 but lost out to Bruce Hornsby and The Range. Several respected American musicians inquired whether they could work with this new talent called Hucknall. He was often dismissive of their overtures: "They're people who previously had careers, but it's as if they're just trying to milk what you've got, take the energy out of you and use it." He turned down a duet with Sam Moore of Sam and Dave fame on the song 'Soul Man' which Lou Reed later accepted.

An offer he could not refuse came from the legendary soul songwriter Lamont Dozier. A former member of the Tamla Motown hit writing machine Holland/Dozier/Holland, it gave Hucknall a chance to trace soul roots to their very source. They spent several days together working on new songs when, in Hucknall's words, Dozier 'banged' the piano and he 'warbled' along. 'Infidelity' and 'Suffer', two tracks spawned from the partnership, eventually found their way on to Simply Red's second album. It allowed Hucknall the pithy indulgence of Hucknall/Dozier/Hucknall on the song writing credits. Two more songs, 'You've Got It' and 'Turn It Up', were included on the band's third album.

Hucknall enjoyed working with Dozier but recognised the roles played by the Holland brothers. "With Lamont, his head is moving so fast. You have to slow him down. He's writing and in the space of five minutes he's working on three separate songs. I was saying, 'Let's just hold on to that one for a moment'. You can imagine the other two guys putting it into order because music just streams out of him. If you don't get it controlled quickly, it's gone. One of the brothers, I hear, was very much concerned with the arrangements and the other the lyrics," he said.

It was gratifying for Hucknall to be accepted into soul's hierarchy. There was no snobbery or disapproval and Bobby Womack told him that when he first heard 'Holding Back The Years' he thought it was sung by Nina Simone. Dozier was so impressed with his enthusiasm that he dubbed him, 'The Right Thing' and inspired the title of the song.

He met Diana Ross and she pecked him on the cheek ("She gave me a kiss - fucking wild!"). The band had appeared on a television show run by Motown in New York. Hucknall was introduced to two of Diana Ross' young daughters and they said they had heard he was 'writing a song for mom'. He took a week's holiday in Florida and wrote 'Shine' and 'Maybe Someday' within the space of two hours. 'Shine' was included on Ross' album of 1987, 'Red Hot Rhythm and Blues'.

Hucknall's reputation had spread to Hollywood and the celebrated director Roman Polanski asked him to contribute music to his film *Frantic*, starring Harrison Ford. The pair dined out in Paris and Polanski asked for a moody piece of music. The moguls contacted Hucknall and asked him to disregard Polanski's wishes - they wanted a strident theme for the opening sequences. Hucknall plundered a song he had written while with The Frantic Elevators, the ballad 'Haven't Got The Power'.

Alex Sadkin, a producer who had worked with a range of performers from James Brown to Grace Jones and Duran Duran, was enlisted for the next Simply Red album. He was chosen primarily for his intrinsic knowledge of reggae music; Hucknall wanted a hard, rootsy sound. After meeting him Hucknall was enthusing about his willingness to experiment. He was a more spontaneous worker than Levine and his *c.v.* was less pop-based. "The original concept with Alex was to go in and record it live. He heard a tape we made in rehearsal and said, 'Well, that sounds great, let's do it like that.' But, not being the sort of band who ever stick to the rules of a concept, we started adding to the sound," said Hucknall. They began recording the second album in October 1986.

The group's following was growing steadily and they were made aware of the devotion they could inspire. Marrtje Oome, a 15-year-old from the Netherlands, left home and travelled to Manchester to be near her favourite group. Her parents contacted newspapers and the police and she was apprehended when she called at a supermarket in Levenshulme, a few miles from Denton, and asked for a job.

Companies wanted to align themselves with Simply Red and the vodka firm Vladivar asked if it could provide sponsorship. Hucknall and Rashman did not want to endorse alcohol and refused the offer. The Coca Cola Company received the same response a year or so later; Hucknall was not a fan of its product.

The 'Picture Book' line up at the 1987 Grammy Awards.

In December 1986 Simply Red were invited to appear at a concert to raise money for the jobless in Manchester called the 'Festival of the Millions'. There were some rumbles of complaint after the band said they were too busy to appear and it hardly helped when Hucknall sent along his infamous hat to raffle.

The single 'The Right Thing' preceded the album and provided an early clue to its content. It had a stronger funk edge than before and Sadkin left the vocal lower in the mix, letting the track run across the tempo created by the thumping bass and choppy guitar. The lyric was a call to arms for men to do 'the right thing' when there was a plea from across the bed during the night. It restored the band's UK chart profile by reaching number 11 and spent six weeks in the Top 40.

The single was the opening track on the album 'Men And Women' released in February 1987, wrapped inside a cover which again showed simply Hucknall, this time in a designer shirt and blowing a kiss to admirers and enemies alike.

'The Right Thing' was followed by the two tracks Hucknall had co-written with Lamont Dozier. 'Infidelity' continued the strong sexual theme where Hucknall announced that he had 'been out loving all night long'. Much like 'The Right Thing', it was a bouncy, up-tempo track with plenty of saxophone fixing together the basic chord progression. Sadkin saw Simply Red in its more rounded form as a group of accomplished musicians rather than as merely a showcase for Hucknall's voice. There was even a photograph of the whole group on the back of the record sleeve to prove it!

The vocals were highlighted, however, on 'Suffer', a modern soul ballad given a warm gospel touch. Hucknall ran through a gamut of vocal skills to instil emotion into an average song. 'I Won't Feel Bad' was a frantic pop/soul tune with too much energy for its own good. The lyric contained whimsical political allusions and in many of the interviews Hucknall was rightly asked to explain throw-away lines like: 'You'll never see me walking down a guilty middle class street.'

The first side closed with a proficient cover of Cole Porter's classic 'Ev'ry Time We Say Goodbye'. It was recorded as a one-off at Stockport's Yellow Two studios and produced by Yvonne Ellis, the studio's resident engineer/producer. It featured the cello playing of Tim Kellett's girlfriend, Eleanor Morris.

It was simply a vehicle for Hucknall's vocal range, recorded in just four hours one spare evening. He crooned easily through the melody, from major to minor, but it was little more than a dip into a rich juke box of material to which he could apply his voice. Ultimately it was a safe option and considering Hucknall's spleen when Alison Moyet covered the Billie Holiday chestnut 'That Ole Devil Called Love', ("I thought it was a sin. I was fucking horrified," he said) it might have been diplomatic not to record the song. It had been scheduled originally as an extra track for inclusion on the B-side of a single but due to its popularity with WEA it made the album.

The flip side was unquestionably Simply Red's most indistinct showcase of material. Sadkin's production, in other places lively and brisk, was heavy-handed and leaden. The side opened with two covers, neither of them particularly strong. Sly Stone's 'Let Me Have It All' was over-long and they veered dangerously close to parody on the version of Bunny Wailer's 'Love Fire'. They did not capture the tight control of the original and their excursion into reggae was no more convincing than another British group flirting with it at the time, Culture Club.

'Move On Out' captured the smooth, slick Philadelphia sound to which it aspired even if it was light of melody. The song was marred by some misplaced guitar doodling from Sylvan Richardson that sounded suspiciously like a solo, a musical technique Hucknall had often lambasted. "They're functional fucking solos. Not self indulgent. It's when they become a meaningless technical drivel for the sake of it," Hucknall protested.

'Shine' was another shapeless and impersonal funk workout which sounded like a rehearsal jam and nothing more substantial. The record closed on a positive note with the aching ballad 'Maybe Someday'. It marked a return to the free, relaxed air of 'Picture Book's' finest moments as Hucknall stretched his larynx across the scales with a telling jazz trumpet breathing steadily in the background. The lyric might well have been written by another celebrated Mancunian, Morrissey, as he pined, 'Maybe one day, someone will come.'

Hucknall later revealed that 'Men And Women' was his least favourite Simply Red album. 'We look back now and think it was a case of that difficult second album. It was aggressive and did not have the warmth of the first one. It really sounds like a touring album; its subject matter is a lot of shagging and general debauchery," he said. AIDS hysteria peaked in 1987 and in the midst of this world-wide backlash against promiscuity Simply Red had appeared with a set of songs eulogising the sexual act. It was timeless rock and soul subject matter, but it might have been wise to make the references more oblique.

'Its subject matter is a lot of shagging and general debauchery'.

Hucknall countered that the record was misinterpreted. He was not advocating free sex, but championing sexual loyalty. "It's very topical because a lot of the tracks are concerned with the value of fidelity. I'm really glad it's called 'Men And Women' because I think it's time people realised they've got a responsibility to themselves to stay alive. I think romance is going to have a real resurgence. Not the Sunsilk advert romance but the real thing - the chase, the idea of seeing someone for three or four weeks without going to bed with them," he told the *News Of The World*.

After 'Men And Women' he appeared regularly in the popular press, usually framed by an attendance of attractive females. He was photographed with the actress Brigitte Nielson and the gossip was that he liked to 'wine and dine her around Paris'. They were also seen together at the Hacienda. The *NME* spotted them: 'Who is the new Rambo in the life of Sylvester Stallone's ex-wife Brigitte Nielson, we hear you ask. We don't? Sod it, we'll tell you anyway. The Silicone Princess was seen at top Manc dancetorium The Hacienda on the arm of... *Mick Hucknall!* Yes, that's right! Mick Out Of *Simply Red*, he with the funny hair and the walking stick affectation.'

The pair hardly matched: she was tall, blonde, statuesque and foreign while he was red, average height and Mancunian. The press loved the incongruity. Their obsession with her silicone-implanted breasts and famous former lovers meant that they, unlike Hucknall, were not privy to her dry humour and charm. "I don't go for the submissive little housewife type with babies dangling from her pinny, pegging out the washing. I go for strident, aggressive types. Older women a lot, yeah," he explained.

Hucknall was picked out by *Melody Maker* as one of the 'Liggers of the Year'. He called often at London's paparazzi emporium, the Limelight club. He was snapped next to a girl named Charlie (sequinned top, painted nails, heavy lipstick) with a blouse swept open to reveal her naked breasts. Hucknall, wine glass before his face, smiled dutifully for the camera. He had waited a long time for the moment; he would soon be bored with it.

In April 1987 Hucknall received a death threat over the telephone at his home in Old Trafford, Manchester. He treated it with commendable contempt. "Come round here and I'll kick your head in," he told the caller.

The other main lyrical concern on 'Men and Women' was politics. He broached it on 'I Won't Feel Bad' and 'Move On Out', a clear message to Margaret Thatcher. Before the band's success Hucknall's position as a Socialist was simple; it was his class's own party, as his father had often told him. During his student days and times as a struggling musician he had regularly issued Marxist dogma but now the

cash was in the other pocket, his own (he was estimated to be a millionaire just a year after the first album's release). "I come from a working class family and there was never any money around. I didn't even travel outside England until I was 21. Right through the first album and on into the promotion period for 'Men And Women' I felt I had to prove something, that I had to justify myself in some way. And it all stemmed from being scared," he said.

He was, for all to see, the tabloid stereotype of a 'champagne Socialist' - he voted Labour and in many photographs there was a glass of effervescent white wine in his hand. He tried, sometimes incoherently, to justify himself but eventually realised it was futile. "What I have learned from listening to a lot of music that has its roots in a rough situation is that I shouldn't have too much of a bee in my bonnet about money and not having any. Those musics are almost an escape from living in shit. Nobody that has been poor actually wants to stay that way. It's only people who have always been comfortable who believe there's anything romantic in hard times," he said.

The *NME*, by tradition left-wing, was not happy with his standpoint. During the General Election campaign of 1987 Hucknall refused to support the Red Wedge movement, a roster of musicians backing the Labour party. 'Such people (musicians) have a responsibility to use their platforms well,' wrote John McCready in his article. It was another prickly interview where Hucknall's frustration boiled over into lively copy. "Listen, there's no fucking Tories in this group. And we're musicians. It's dangerous. I'm up here to deal with music, not tell a bunch of fucking kids whose side they should be on. When I was a kid politicians were just those fuckers on the telly who spoiled the cartoons," he said.

Hucknall wanted it both ways. He was happy to inject his lyrics with rhetoric and criticise the Conservative Party but would not commit himself to Labour apart from with his vote. There was a belief in 1987 that Margaret Thatcher's tenure was to finish and many socialists were disappointed when one of their famous supporters was struck down by uncharacteristic coyness.

Unavoidably, Hucknall often contradicted himself. In one interview he was critical of expensive designer clothing, especially suits designed by Paul Smith. A few years later his group were wearing them. "I work with him now because as a band we get a brilliant discount. I always shop in places where I get money knocked off. It's ridiculous what I do; I'll go somewhere else if it's two pence cheaper. I still feel guilty if I get a taxi. I've still got that Paul Smith suit... and I wear it! He makes fucking good clothes. When I was slagging them off I thought I was being a big rebel, a street kid, being real. I now know that I'm real anyway, and I don't have to act it," he said.

'I go for strident, aggressive types. Older women a lot, yeah'.

'Men And Women' made number two in the UK albums chart in March 1987 but did less well in the US where it stalled at 31. Unlike in the UK, where a brace of hit singles could translate immediately into healthy album sales, the US showing was typical in a commercial field that took many years to infiltrate.

In the US the second album considerably under-sold 'Picture Book' which had shifted more than a million copies. In other territories, Europe especially, the band's profile grew at a healthy pace and sales of both 'Picture Book' and 'Men And Women' eventually broke the three million barrier.

'My dislike of all the promotional stuff never went away, it just got worse…'

It was noteworthy that 'Picture Book' sold strongly as a back-catalogue record in the UK and after the release of 'Men And Women' it reached its highest chart position of number two. It was tangible proof that Simply Red had longevity. Their records had passed the ultimate test - the public was buying them as birthday and Christmas presents.

At the end of February 1987 Simply Red embarked on the 'Men And Women' tour of the UK and Ireland. In Manchester they played two concerts at the Apollo Theatre to meet demand and from March 23 to 26 they had a run of shows at London's Hammersmith Odeon.

There was a change in Simply Red's line-up after the tour. The departure of Sylvan Richardson in the autumn of 1987 was the first alteration for more than two years. His place was taken by Aziz Ibrihim, another Manchester musician, and the band was also augmented by Ian Kirkham, the Preston-born saxophonist who had played with them since the tour to promote 'Picture Book'.

On the tour to promote 'Men And Women' Richardson decided that he no longer wished to be part of Simply Red. He was tired of the promotional treadmill. "I hated it, so much. I remember doing *Wogan* and Mick and Elliot said, 'Right, you've got to dance'. I felt extremely uncomfortable. I tapped my foot a bit. I'm a musician not a dancer. It was doing my head in, I wanted to get away from that showbiz thing. I was thinking, 'I'm not put on the planet to do this'. My dislike of all the promotional stuff never went away, it just got worse. It was at saturation point and I was very unhappy," said Richardson.

The surviving band members queued up to explain his departure in the group's official fanzine: "There's a basic philosophy with this group that everyone pulls their weight, and no one here among us felt that Sylvan was pulling his weight as a performer on stage or as a person regarding promoting TV and radio," Hucknall was quoted as saying. "Sylvan was very disinterested in that side of what we were doing and you have to be willing to do everything," said Kellett. "When we played live we had to compensate for Sylvan for over a year because there was a hole where he was standing. There was nothing happening and there was nothing to look at from the audience's point of view," added McIntyre.

Richardson had been uncomfortable with the aura around the group, Hucknall and Rashman's grip was too firm: it had stopped being fun. "I didn't like what I was seeing or the way I felt and it forced me into a shell. I was learning about the business end of it on the spot. Elliot was very shrewd. Mostly, for me, it was Mick and Elliot, it was very unnerving - they were the wheel within the wheel and everybody was trying to get on the inside, trying to keep on the good side of Mick and Elliot," he said.

Quiet, unassuming and a musical purist, Richardson was the antithesis of Hucknall. While Hucknall could be said to share the same commitment to music, he also possessed the business nous to understand the need to push and shove. "Mick speaks his mind, even though when I was working with him I could not handle it. He just says whatever he wants, but that's his strength as well. He acts and does and says as he pleases," he said.

The Simply Red brass boys,
Kirkham (left) and Kellett.

In hindsight the guitarist felt he was too precious, too serious, too pious: it had all come too soon. He was the Homeboy, staying in his room reading the Bible (he was a Jehovah's Witness) while the rest were in the hotel bar. "I think they thought I was a bit of a weirdo. I was very religious at the time which didn't help at all. I was looking down my nose at everyone's lifestyle. I felt out of place, or was made to feel out of place. I don't know whether it was my age or my character. I was very quiet, all the time. I spoke when I was spoken to," he said.

He wanted to return to his first instrument, the bass guitar, and on leaving the group studied classical composition with the highly-respected musician Edgar Grana in New York. He was to stay within the So What Arts stable, there was talk of setting up a record label called A.S.A.P to release his solo records. "There was a lot of tension because we had never talked about anything properly. I had bottled it all up, I had two years' worth of bottled-up anger. In retrospect it was wrong. In my life now I try and be more forthwith, whatever I feel I try and deal with it at that time. I was out of my wits in Simply Red. I didn't feel safe, a lost little boy, that is how I felt the whole time," he said.

He returned to Manchester and regular session work with renowned jazz figures like Andy Sheppard. He was, on his own terms, fulfilling an original plan to become an ace session player. He formed his own group, named after himself, and played solidly on the jazz circuit. They recorded two tracks for a Blue Note compilation album and Richardson was at last happy in his musical environment, though there was a period of adjustment. "I was pissed off for a while, I kind of got through that. I'm doing what I want to do, to write and play. I'm not an élitist or muso any more. I've come of age."

Time also lent Richardson a new perspective on Simply Red. He saw them as a distinctive commercial force, brilliantly organised and executed, if not playing his favourite type of music. "I couldn't stand being around Mick most of the time but, in a way, I have always been fond of him as well. I have had a chance to get away from it all and think about it. It must be the same for other people in that he is a pain sometimes, but underneath all that he is trying to do his art, which he is very good at," he said.

Aziz Ibrihim, born of Pakistani parents and brought up in Longsight, Manchester, was a bright, lively character. While he studied for a university degree he played basketball at a high level and also found that he had a talent for guitar playing. He could adapt effortlessly to any musical style and was in demand on the local circuit. He was, amazingly in the circumstances, invited to join Simply Red before either Hucknall, Rashman and Dodd had met him, heard him play, or even asked him to audition. "We have heard a lot of good things about you," he was told over the phone by Dodd. And that was it.

The Simply Red rhythm section:
Bowers and Joyce (right).

He attended a two-day rehearsal to learn the songs with the other musicians. At the end of the second day he finally met

'You can't use that in this band'.

Hucknall. The singer stared at him intensely and then spoke: "Do you like curry?" He said that he did and then Hucknall saw his guitar, a pink Ibanez. "You can't use that in this band," he was told. From that audacious introduction, Ibrihim was aware of a tension, an awkwardness that he articulated to the man he had replaced and who was also a good friend. "It is a very odd group..." warned Richardson.

In the summer of 1987 two unofficial picture discs were released carrying interviews with Hucknall. The first appeared on the Baktabak label in May and the other on Tell Tales Records in September.

Simply Red's singles chart form remained erratic. 'Infidelity' was not strong enough to stand out as a single and its journey upwards ended at number 31 in June 1987. It meant that after the release of eight singles the band had still not had two consecutive Top 30 hits.

WEA cut its losses and quickly issued another single. As the up-tempo 'Infidelity' had not won favour, it tried the jazzy, downbeat 'Maybe Someday' instead. There was almost nil response; it was hardly played on the radio and for the first time ever a Simply Red single did not chart.

It caused only minor concern at the label because it was convinced 'Men And Women' contained another hit single. The Cole Porter standard 'Ev'ry Time We Say Goodbye', with its loyalty to the original, was an almost sure-fire hit. It had already been discovered by many DJs - it just needed to be showcased as a single in its own right.

There was an obvious reluctance on the band's behalf to rely on another cover version, it would have equated to four hits, two of them covers. Once the decision was made, WEA gave it full backing by releasing five formats of the single and in the chart announced on Boxing Day of 1987 Simply Red were standing proud at number 11.

The single significantly expanded Simply Red's fan base. While it further alienated them from *Smash Hits* readers - a frivolous, ephemeral market anyway - it crossed them over to an older age group, people who enjoyed the gentle refrains of Radio Two. The record also provided Hucknall with a degree of classicism. Mick Hucknall and Cole Porter? A few years earlier it was an absurd marriage of styles and personalities, but not any more.

The band toured the US in the autumn of 1987 and there was still a determination to develop a following in the country. The venues were much smaller than in Europe, some with a capacity of about 1,000, and four shows did not sell out. "Financially we were losing a fortune and we forfeited most of the royalties from 'Men and Women' to pay for the tour," said Rashman.

The smaller audiences meant Hucknall could give people the personal touch. Mira Coleman, a fan from California, had given him a rose outside a venue when he last visited. He remembered her when he returned a year later. "That's what I like about Mick - he's just like you and me, he's not full of himself," she said.

In the UK 1987 had been notable for the chart domination held by the production team of Stock, Aitken and Waterman. The trio had brought brash, synthetic pop to the public through performers like Rick Astley, Mel and Kim and Sinitta and more were on the way. Simply Red should have been the antidote. Unfortunately, the evidence was that the band's singles were not consistent: none had made the Top 10 during the year despite the extensive advertising, touring and promotional strength of WEA.

There were still clues to future promise: sales of the album were strong and 'Men And Women' was the 19th best-selling LP of the year behind a formidable list including Michael Jackson, U2, Paul McCartney and Fleetwood Mac. It was clear to WEA that Simply Red were becoming an 'albums band'. It was where the greater profit lay so there was no alarm at the sporadic success of the singles.

chapter 6

Recording and touring commitments had been heavy throughout 1987 and a break was essential, mainly to write new material. 'Men and Women' had been heavily plundered and by the release of 'I Won't Feel Bad' in February 1988 and its dismal chart showing of 68, the band had more than a slightly jaded look to it. They took 1988 as a year of recuperation, playing just a handful of shows in Spain and Portugal.

Hucknall's ambition of establishing himself as both a singer and songwriter of note was only half accomplished. The majority of his own songs had flopped as singles and three years after Simply Red's first release none of the songs written by him since then had actually made the UK Top 10. He remained patient, willing to learn the techniques of the artform.

The chance to work again with producer Alex Sadkin was ruled out when he was killed in a car crash. The band decided to revert back to the warm sound of their début album and enlisted the help of Stewart Levine again. "Stewart and I have a very special friendship and very similar tastes in music. He's a very musical person - one, I think, of a dying breed of producers whose talent is based upon a sense of music more than just a technical sense," said Hucknall.

The budget was bigger than ever before and they flew to the West Indies to record at the famous Air Studios in Montserrat. During the spring of 1988, the band partly re-located to Milan. On his travels, Hucknall had spent time in the northern Italian city and the relaxed, cosmopolitan ambience was seductive. He bought a flat in Gallarate, a 40-minute drive out of the city, for a sum reported to be in excess of £300,000. The other group members had adjoining apartments and there was a room on the floor above used for rehearsal. The UK press now had a reason to berate Hucknall - he was a tax exile.

The *Daily Mirror*, historically affiliated to the soft Left of UK politics, struck first. 'Soul Loses Its Voices' ran the headline and it reported that Hucknall had bought a luxury flat in Milan at the cost of a cool million and it had a 500 square foot kitchen. He pretended otherwise, but Hucknall was hurt at his portrayal by the UK media. "The *Daily Mirror* article was hilarious. Do you know how big 500 square foot is? It'd take 10 minutes

Ruby Blues

'Soul Loses Its Voices'.

Stewart Levine considered himself a musical Mr Fix-it with an unspoken duty to bring together musicians whom he thought would suit each other. He had just finished working with a top Brazilian musician, Ivan Lins, and had been impressed with the guitarist he used, Heitor Terxeira Pereira. He recommended him to Hucknall and in the summer of 1988 he became the band's newest member and they abbreviated his name to Heitor T.P.

He was well-versed in Latin rhythms and widely respected as a first-rate musician, if not Brazil's finest guitarist. He was raised in a musical family in Rio and left to study music in Boston, Massachusetts, before releasing two solo albums in his own country. He was 24 when he joined Simply Red and moved with his wife and two children to live in London. "There is a rawness and craziness here which America has lost. There it has become too polished. I like the British attitude to music," he explained.

Aziz Ibrihim had spent under a year in Simply Red, during which time he reportedly earned £50,000 as a session player. His departure was blamed on the almost-obligatory 'musical differences' and he returned, disgruntled, to the Manchester session circuit. "I soon noticed that everyone in the group was acting strange. There wasn't any sense of camaraderie. On tour, most of the time, everyone tended to act in a peculiar manner. In a kind of, 'Don't touch me, don't come near me... I'm a really weird guy, I'm a genius.' It was the strangest thing," he said.

Ibrihim had found the group to be built on cliques and a servitude to Hucknall's ego. "Mick Hucknall had absolutely no idea how to treat other human beings. It never entered his head that he might actually gain something by learning how they feel, by finding out how they wished to express themselves," he said.

His presence in the group hardly had time to register with fans although, in contrast to Richardson, his on-stage enthusiasm had logged with Rashman who felt it distracted too much attention from Hucknall. He told the guitarist to keep the parts simple and close his legs while he played them!

to walk from one side to the other. If they could only see what we're actually living in. And to say I've become a recluse is utterly ridiculous. I've been rehearsing. I've been to Montserrat to make an album. Nothing could be further from the truth," he said.

In reality, the group still had their roots in the north west of England. Chris Joyce bought a house in Heaton Chapel, near Stockport, Tim Kellett lived in Trafford and McIntyre was hoping to settle in the area. Only Tony Bowers had made a definite commitment to Italy; he married a girl called Antonella from Milan and they had a child together. Hucknall maintained his modest semi-detached house near Manchester city centre but since it had been burgled eight times during 1987, homecomings were becoming memorable for the wrong reasons. Also, as it was a local landmark, he had to have every window covered with metal blinds, even when he was inside.

Ibrihim became, as the years rolled on and his memory fermented, a regular source of embarrassment to Simply Red. In January 1993, for instance, he sold his story to the *North West Sunday News and Echo*. Under the sub-heading of 'My Naughty Nights On The Road With Pop Star Mick' he plundered his memory for tales of suitable scurrility. "One time when we were rehearsing, Mick boasted to me, 'Remember those two tarts I was talking to last night? Well I had both of them'," said Ibrihim. He also said Hucknall's nickname was, 'Dick Fuck All' after he had been seen with more than 100 women on the tour. Obviously So What needed to vet its employees with greater diligence in the future.

Simply Red marked their comeback in January 1989 with the single 'It's Only Love', a drastic improvement on the run of shapeless singles of a year earlier. The most dynamic aspect of this vibrant number was a new-found confidence. The snag was that it was another cover version. Written by Jimmy and Vella Cameron, it originally appeared as a B-side on a Barry White single.

It reached number 13 in the UK but did not receive the same positive response in the US where it scraped into the Top 60. It was apparent that they were struggling to maintain their early impact across the Atlantic.

The cover shot of the new album 'A New Flame' featured just Hucknall, bent forwards with his long hair falling in copper spirals so that it completely obscured his face. He was now world famous, the red hair was enough. There was no need to actually show his face. "We've always made it clear that it was a concerted decision by all the members of the group that we should do that, because it's more reliable to just have one person on the thing rather than five people and also because I look more recognisable. It doesn't affect the relationship with the band, because it wasn't as if we started out with a group picture on the first album and then the record company decided, 'Oh we'll pick Mick out. It doesn't work like that," said Hucknall.

'A New Flame' saw the band come of age. Compared with the previous two albums, this was a sustained melodic attack. Stewart Levine's touch on the mixing desk was light and there was no reliance on studio gloss or gimmickry to mask a shortage of ideas. The songs, in the main, were pruned to a tight pop format which still allowed the character of the group, personified by Hucknall's voice, to shine through.

It opened with 'It's Only Love', a track already familiar from which emanated warmth and personality. It glorified new love, relayed across a stop-start time signature. It was a pointed response to the critics - it neither 'borrowed' from classic soul numbers nor relied heavily on Hucknall's voice to pull it through.

'Remember those two tarts I was talking to last night? Well I had both of them'.

In earlier work Hucknall sometimes squeezed too much from his vocal cords and it gave it an unnecessary histrionic touch. 'You've Got It', another track co-written with Lamont Dozier, showcased his development as a singer. The pitch throughout the well-paced ballad was perfect and there was none of the showy emotion of before.

Kirkham, now promoted so that his photograph was included in the album packaging, formed a pulsating brass duo with Tim Kellett on the funky 'To Be With You'. As Hucknall listed the itinerary for his new female friend (be with, talk with, sleep with, make love with), the bass slapped, the guitar chopped and the drums splashed. In the best traditions of a Prince-style funk House Party, it caught a group clearly enjoying themselves.

If the opening four tracks had discreet influences, it was obvious from where 'More' originated. Opening with a spoken cod-Rasta introduction of, 'We used to meet from time to time, up in the mountains,' it developed into a full-blown excursion through the light dub style of Gregory Isaacs. Apart from the ostentatious muzak guitar solo (and it *was* a solo), it was a winning re-interpretation. The smell of ganja was in the air and Moss Side and Kingston did not seem all that far apart.

Hucknall returned to a political theme on 'Turn It Up'. He was again re-claiming Britain for the under-class. The horns blared in the best Philadelphia mode and the track, much like 'To Be With You', was another blistering funk outing.

His lyric writing, especially on the theme of love, had matured and there was little of the bluntness of before. 'Love Lays Its Tune' captured him at his most sensitive and sentimental. The seductive ballad was an 'album track' but not in the sense of mere filler material. It was relaxed, deliberated music designed to be showcased within a larger body of work.

His old adversary, Prime Minister Margaret Thatcher, was clearly under attack in 'She'll Have To Go'. The aggressive politics were delivered in a smooth pop package. He took several lyrical liabilities ('I was born on the pavement') and dusted down several clichés but at least the statement was unambiguous.

In a radio interview he issued Utopian rhetoric, even showing a benign attitude to Conservatism. "I don't close myself off to anybody. It is probably a good thing to have people on the Right - it's not about getting rid of all the people that don't agree with what you're saying, it's about all coming to a decision where you've got to live together despite your differences, so I've no problem with anybody. I think there would be a wonderful irony, say at a disco at a Tory party conference, if they all stood there dancing to 'Money's Too Tight (To Mention)'. I wouldn't mind, I've nothing against them, I do not know them as people, you know." The young and intolerant Hucknall would have seethed by the radio had he heard such bland diplomacy.

The album's cover version was Harold Melvin and The Blue Notes' 'If You Don't Know Me By Now'. It had reached number nine in the UK chart of February 1973 and Simply Red's version was fairly loyal to the original, a no-nonsense delivery, earnest without being mawkish and expertly produced by Levine.

'Enough', written by Hucknall in collaboration with Joe Sample of The Crusaders, closed the record in low-key mood. The production, for once, was flat and it floundered in the new spirit of under-statement as the keyboards, brass and guitar meandered.

The album was released in February 1989, nearly two years after 'Men And Women', and for the first time Simply Red made the number one spot in the UK chart. It entered the chart at the top and stayed there for a month, returning to number one on two subsequent occasions.

In press interviews Hucknall referred to it as a 'love' record, compared with the sexual drive of its predecessor. "All I can say is that the songs are the truth, so whether it's about me or someone else is irrelevant, because it's the truth; it's definitely about somebody," he said.

It was widely thought that most of the lyrics centred on his flourishing relationship with an American model named Dee. Hucknall had met the intelligent, fair-haired Texan when Simply Red appeared in Tokyo. He contacted her when they played her hometown of Dallas and afterwards she was his constant companion on the tour bus. She was introduced to Reg Hucknall and Aunty Nellie on a visit to Denton. They were together for several months in various cities around the world before their careers and the distance between pulled them apart.

On his promotional tour of the UK Hucknall was repeatedly asked to cover old themes - his 'arrogance'; his status as a 'tax exile'; his alleged promiscuity; his Socialist beliefs; his wealth; his whiteness. "Instead of taking an aggressive stance or feeling threatened by the media in Britain, I feel that we don't have anything to defend, we don't need to be defensive, because they ain't so fucking great either. If we're a crap band, then we're a crap band. We feel we have nothing to prove any more and we feel more relaxed," he said.

Simply Red had, from 'Picture Book' until Richardson's exit, contained two black men but the fact that the band had largely been one third black was overlooked. "The tragedy was that two members of the group were black, it was almost like calling them white. Because I was the frontman I was made the scapegoat. It did matter that they were black, it does matter that I'm white but I also can't escape what music I've been brought up on, what I love. I can understand their criticisms and their snobberies but from the position I'm in I've just got to ignore it because I've got to get on with what I'm doing," said Hucknall. McIntyre and Richardson, for their part, were pleased to work with a white musician willing to cite black performers as a major influence.

'I thought it was the coolest thing I'd ever seen'.

While it was undeniable that Hucknall's songs adhered loyally to the tone and phrasing of American black music, he was, like every other performer, undertaking a process of assimilation: he just happened to be very good at it. "This white soul boy tag that comes with Simply Red - as the years go on and on I start to find it more and more ridiculous and absolutely amazing. What is Elvis Presley? What is John Lennon? What are The Rolling Stones? What are every single white artist that has ever been? Deep Purple, Led Zeppelin, they are all entrenched in black music completely. All their first records were basic imitations of black music," he said in a radio interview in 1992.

His anger was understandable. He had aspired for years to be part of an international musicians' culture. He idolised a style that belonged to a long-gone era of battered guitar cases, early morning trains to Mississippi, crumpled old suits, plectrums held between teeth. It was painful beyond words to be told that not only was he not part of it, but he had actually exploited it. He was a tribute to the black artist, not a plagiarist. And he had his own blues, born and raised on northern streets without a mother's love.

The rendition of 'If You Don't Know Me By Now' was released as a single and made number two in the UK chart. It did even better in the US when it topped the *Billboard* 100 for one week in June. It was a boost to sales in the States and the album moved up to number 22 and stayed in the Top 100 for an impressive 39 weeks.

There was a violent incident at Simply Red's show at Wembley Arena when one of their fans, Jim Murray of Kennington, London, was attacked by security staff. He alleged that he was set upon by four men who punched and kicked him until he was unconscious. The band promised to back him if it gave rise to a court case: 'If it turns out to be a genuine cause for complaint the band will have no hesitation in supporting and assisting the injured party in bringing action against those concerned,' read the official statement.

The assault was not typical of a Simply Red concert. The band generally inspired a warm, peaceful atmosphere. "Our audience ranges from about 15 years of age to 50. They just seem to mix with each other so well. There's never any trouble at the gigs or violence. They seem to be such a convivial group of people. It creates an atmosphere that is fantastic," said Hucknall.

On the tour for 'A New Flame' Simply Red were supported by Manchester group Distant Cousins, managed by former *City Life* journalist Chris Paul. They had been chosen despite offers of a 'buy-on' from record companies, some willing to pay up to

£20,000 for its act to accompany Simply Red. It was clearly a gesture by Hucknall. "They were great to us, we were well fed and they lent a lot of technical assistance. We didn't pay them anything," said Paul.

Word filtered through, however, that Hucknall was displeased. The band were performing an acoustic set and he wanted drums and bass. "We were getting messages every day that Mick wasn't happy. We had not rehearsed as a full group and could not afford to hire new people. Besides, the shows were going down well from our point of view. They started to say that we would not go to Europe with the tour if we didn't change the line-up," said Paul. Distant Cousins did not cross the channel with Simply Red.

During the summer Hucknall made another style statement to rank alongside the walking cane and cape as a focus of ridicule. He spent six hours in a dentist's chair having a perfectly healthy tooth removed to be replaced by a false one with a ruby embedded in it. The treatment cost $1,000 and was carried out by a dentist friend in Los Angeles. It had been a secret ambition since childhood after he had seen the blues musician Buddy Guy with one. "I thought it was the coolest thing I'd ever seen," he said.

Hucknall was doing his own thing and did not care if it was seen as tacky or ostentatious. "As far as I'm concerned I just wear what I want, and look the way I want. I always wore what the fuck I wanted, sometimes it was mad and sometimes it was just ordinary. I still feel the same way. There's charges made that it's gimmickry, but what do you need gimmicks for? I don't need gimmicks," he said.

As well as the clothes and adornments, the media kept a scrupulous watch over the Hucknall physique. His was not the svelte form expected of a pop star and he was reminded of this quite frequently. 'Amply Fed' was a common nickname as the jackets became baggier, apparently to hide an expanding stomach. "I'm totally into food in a very heavy way," he admitted. "It's not a matter of quantity, it's just about taking an interest. I put a lot of weight on at one stage because I was boozing a lot. Eating a lot as well and not getting much chance to exercise. It's just a phase you go through. Also when I gave up smoking there's a general thing that you put weight on. Me old man was the same."

The tour to promote 'A New Flame' was extensive and apart from the occasional week off before moving to another country, it lasted for more than a year, effectively taking up the whole of 1989 and ending finally in March 1990. When it was completed Hucknall saw the importance of pacing the group. "I realised that it was starting to feel very systematic, I really didn't want to go through all that again, so I decided to pull out for a while," he said. Simply Red, like most major league pop and rock artists, were about to work in a rough three or four year cycle: album, tour, year-off, write and record.

Rashman revealed tentative plans to form his own record label through which he could nurture new talent. The first stage in establishing 'House of Chaos' was in July 1989 when he moved a 16-track studio from his home in Didsbury, Manchester, to a rehearsal room in Denton. "Creative people need a medium to work on that's low on overheads," he told reporters. The label was not heard of again.

There was further evidence of Rashman's itchiness to vary his workload when, in 1989, he briefly took on the management of another Manchester band, James. Famously idiosyncratic, James, from the very outset, seemed a peculiar band to call upon Rashman's services. Although concealed, James had big plans and believed Rashman was better suited than Martine MacDonagh who had, quite ably, managed the band until that point.

As expected, the liaison floundered. James' frontman, Tim Booth, was prickly in the field of band/label relations and would not play the corporate game. He clashed with Rashman and on the final parting reportedly cried: 'I'm not one of your plastic pop star puppets.' Rashman remembered the histrionic line and sent Booth a fax containing it, when, just a few years later, James, under MacDonagh's guidance once more, scored a string of hit singles.

Hucknall was willing to eschew pop star security paranoia and reactivated his Black Rhythms disco at Manchester's Ritz club. Every Tuesday during November 1989 he climbed into the DJ's booth at the city centre club and plugged in his portable DAT machine.

The tapes had earlier been lovingly assembled at home. He took over the DJ's role at clubs throughout the world when the mood took.

While Simply Red made their way around the world, WEA released a steady stream of singles. The title track from the album was issued in July 1989, and backed by a distinctive video it made number 17 in the UK charts.

In a bid to continue the momentum, WEA again made the mistake of releasing one single too many from the album. 'It's Only Love', 'If You Don't Know Me By Now' and 'A New Flame' had each been Top 20 hits and it amounted to Simply Red's most consistent chart run.

While 'You've Got It' was a strong ballad and blended in perfectly on the album, it was not distinctive enough to

Friend of the stars. Hucknall with Tanita Tikaram.

'Another crock of unmitigated bison shite from Simply Red's astonishingly banal 'A New Flame' album'.

merit single release. WEA tried valiantly to bolster it with a live acoustic recording of 'Holding Back The Years' on the B-side along with several different formats. In November 1989 it lumbered up the UK charts before halting at number 46. The *NME*, unremorseful as ever, slavered: 'Another crock of unmitigated bison shite from Simply Red's astonishingly banal 'A New Flame' album.'

In February 1990 Simply Red were awarded a Grammy at the 32nd annual awards at the Shrine Auditorium in Los Angeles. Their version of 'If You Don't Know Me By Now' was voted 1989's best rhythm and blues song.

Hucknall wanted to spend 1990 travelling and deciphering the catastrophic changes affecting the world. "It was a period when a lot of things were happening. The Berlin Wall came down - all of a sudden everyone just felt positive, like 'My God, this is the dawning of a new age'. What was that George Bush statement? A very silly statement really, 'a new World Order' - that was very naïve. Didn't even think about the problems that were befalling the Soviet Union. And then Saddam came along and it all just went 'Uuuuuuuuh!' - the bottom fell out. It was all so wonderful, and then, suddenly they're going to war! And it's like 'What is Kuwait?'," he said.

chapter 7

Shock waves rippled across middle-Europe and the Middle East in 1990. It was a year of change and Mick Hucknall watched enthralled from his position of part-Milan, part-Manchester. He wanted a similar transition in Simply Red. It had, he felt, become too predictable, too samey, an edge was missing.

"At the end of the 'New Flame' tour I was still stuck within the confines of it. It started to feel like a prison, having that kind of band where you're rigidly stuck with musicians, whether you think they've grown or not. And when you have a band like that sometimes musicians simply don't grow at the same rate as you do. Their ideas are not as creative. And yet some of them are. And the ones you relate to, the ones that you see growing, you wanna keep, and the ones that are lagging behind, or have gone off into their own musical travels, it's time to make a change," he said.

It was rockspeak and its translation was obvious - the frontman was about to fire the band, or part of it. In Hucknall's case it was the latter. "It really coincided with me realising that

All For The Music

I wanted to keep Simply Red as a bubbling thing, a rolling thing, where people come and go. You keep like a solid base, and one or two people change per album. They might go on to do better things, they might go on to fade into obscurity, but whatever they do, you've given them the best shot they're going to get. Most of my musicians will tell you that you don't get better than this. Our structure on the road, certainly what they get paid, their facilities and the fact that they're looked after - it doesn't come better than this," he told Ireland's *Hot Press*.

Insiders believed Pereira's introduction and easy assimilation into Simply Red had set Hucknall on a train of thought. The guitarist was one of the world's finest players in his field, so why shouldn't the same high level of expertise stretch to the others?

'What they get paid, their facilities and the fact that they're looked after - it doesn't come better than this'.

The players who had not 'grown' with Hucknall were the rhythm section of drummer Chris Joyce and bassist Tony Bowers. "I really didn't have much of a problem dealing with Tony, our relationship had pretty much broken down. But I had a problem with Chris because I really like Chris. But you have to say to yourself, just like anybody in any kind of work, whether it be like a business or artistic work, you have to say, 'What are you doing? I'm making music and I want to make the best music that I can make'," said Hucknall.

Sylvan Richardson had stayed in touch with the group and was amazed to learn of the sackings. "It was the biggest shock of my life; these were Mick's blood-brothers, I thought. It was a total shock. Chris had worked very hard, and Tony did. I think Chris actually worked the hardest, digging his heels in and playing his heart out a lot of the time. It was part of Mick's masterplan and maybe Chris did not fit in any more. All of a sudden he was the accessory that he always was. Everybody there is an accessory, no matter how you cut the cake, but when you're there at the time you don't see it that way," he said.

Hucknall had often spoken of the immortality music provided. To him the legacy was more important than the people, problems and processes that supplied it. He was solemn on the issue: "I have to get on with the music. The music's gonna be here when I'm dead and gone, so you really have got to take your best shot with the music. That's how strongly I feel about it really."

He was listening increasingly to modern dance music and wanted a stronger edge to Simply Red. The rhythm section, in his opinion, was not 'up to the job'. Their departure again focused attention on Hucknall's dominant role but he was unambiguous: "This is a solo career and it always has been but it's taken me five years to realise it. No, I just don't like the name Mick Hucknall very much. I was in Chicago once and this black guy came up to me and said, 'Yo! Simply! How you doing my man? Well, see you Mr Red!'"

It was evident that Hucknall's dictatorial role had developed over the years. The settled line-up of himself, Kellett, McIntyre, Joyce, Richardson and Bowers had considered themselves a group and not a backing band. In an interview with journalist Johnny Waller in 1987 Chris Joyce had said: "Internally, we *do* work as a group and Mick is the face that sells the group. It would have been too difficult to get people to know six faces at the start - it's just too much for them to take in." Joyce compared the band-singer relationship as similar to that of Talking Heads, The Rolling Stones or U2. He was out of synchronisation with Hucknall's view and so was Kellett who added: "The people that are really into the music look at us as a band. But from a marketing point of view, why not use his hair and face?"

If the group had seen the constant promotion of Hucknall as a cosmetic, irrelevant factor they had deluded themselves.

By agreeing to focus on his features they were inadvertently eroding their own importance. "Has anybody ever known who the other people in Simply Red were? I haven't. And have they ever cared? No. The whole branding of the group is around Mick. They're not John, Paul, George and Ringo, never have been. The way people use it as a sort of criticism, that Mick's more ruthless than other musicians, it's just sentimental claptrap," said journalist Mark Cooper.

Former members claimed they had been misled by the eloquence of Rashman and Hucknall. "I was fooled at first," said Richardson. "There was all this talk of camaraderie and solidarity, 'We are a band, do this, and do this together, but the words and actions didn't fit, and the feeling. There wasn't any band, it was Mick and the boys. I couldn't come to terms with it. Why say that? If Mick had said, 'You guys are just pawns in a game' I could have understood it."

There had been more than a murmur of dissatisfaction over the distribution of song writing royalties within the group. It had remained unresolved since the early days. "It was something tossed around a few times. The advance was split eight ways when I was in the group (between each musician and Rashman and Dodd) but Mick got the publishing which was where the real money was. There was a lot of input from the band on a lot of tunes. I've heard it's still a problem. I hear Fritz's influence, for instance, all over the music but I do not see his name in the credits. It's still happening, on a bigger scale now because there's more money involved," said Richardson.

Hucknall did not waver from his main theme - everything was sacrificial to the music: "I don't think I'm tyrannical at all. I didn't like losing people that I'd known for so long and grown up with as friends. But I had to make a definite decision about

whether or not I wanted to leave some kind of accurate representation of everything I wanted to achieve with my music. I didn't start the band simply to be with friends, I wanted to leave my little piece of history," he explained.

He drew once more from the swamp of black American musical history to find his metaphor. He wasn't James Brown, fining his band when they hit the wrong note or came in a bar late. "I'm not a control freak; this isn't a Prince situation. The people I work with I try to give some creative space. I'm like an old band leader, providing a springboard for musicians who can come and go as they grow or fade," he told *The Sunday Times*.

'Has anybody ever known who the other people in Simply Red were?'

In media terms there were two Mick Hucknalls. In mainland Europe he was a virtuoso, an artiste worthy of great respect. On the other side of the English Channel journalists were still sniffing out trivia in his laundry basket and school reports. At a press conference in Montreux, Switzerland Hucknall was bombarded with questions by UK reporters about the life of a tax exile; a poor man become rich and a womaniser. An indignant German reporter stood up: "Can we have some questions about the fact that Mick Hucknall is a musician?" Hucknall nodded in enthusiastic agreement while the British hacks shook their heads.

Hucknall with Herbie Hancock
and Pete Townshend.

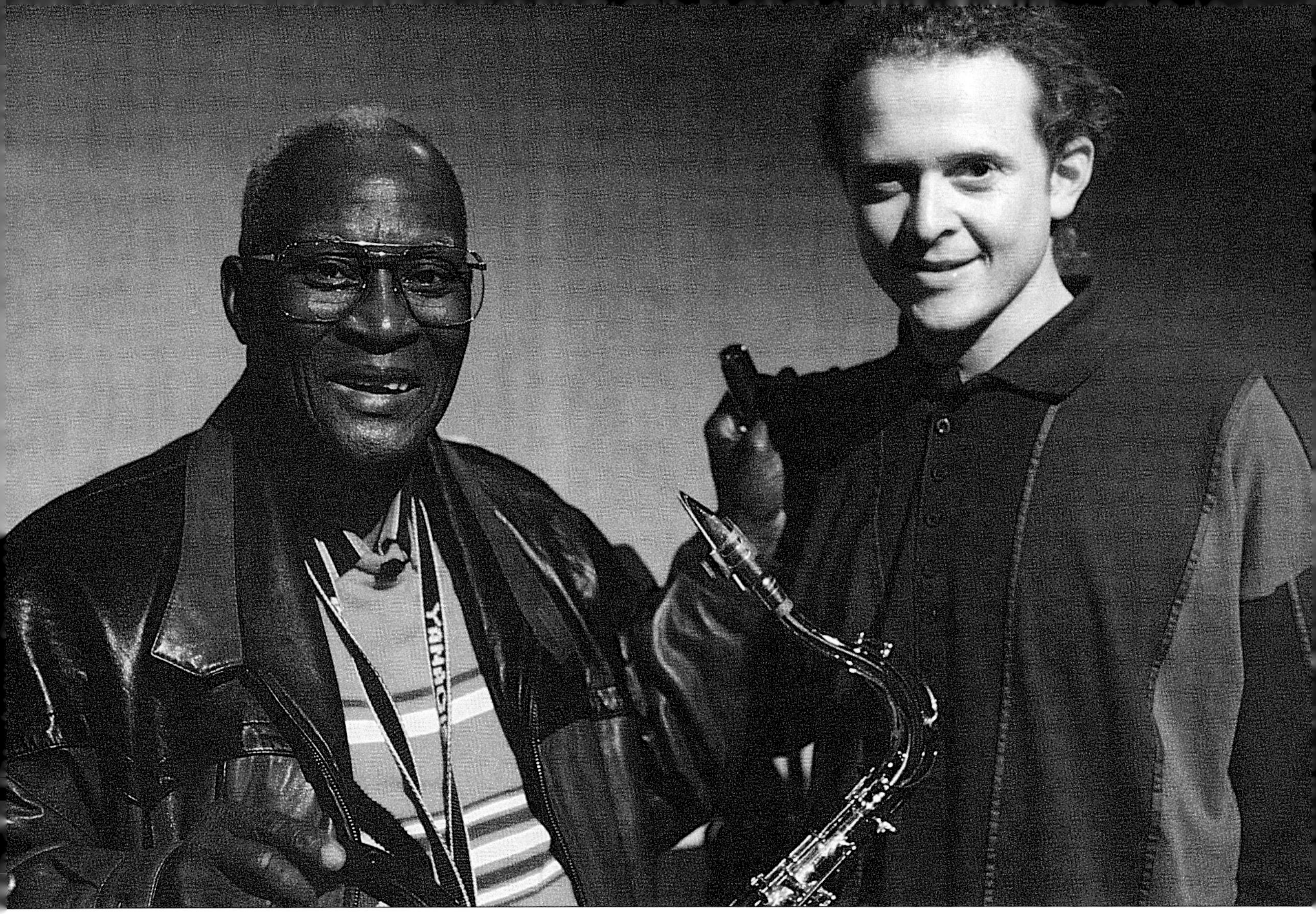

Top:
Hucknall with saxophonist Andy Hamilton in January 1991.

Below:
Singing with bluesman Andy Brown.

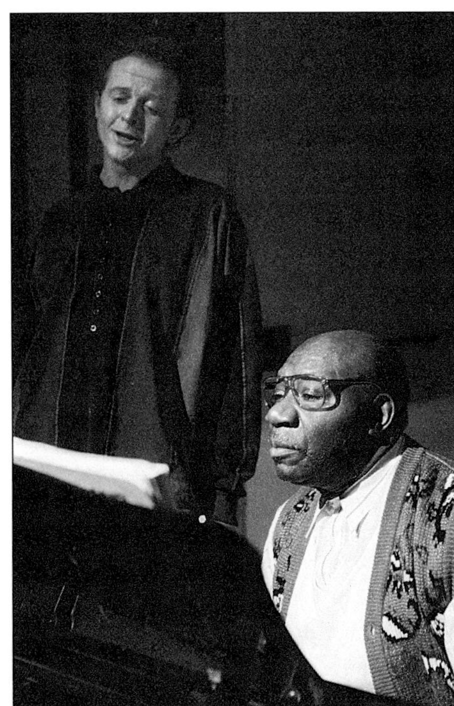

He accepted several offers of work during his sabbatical leave but maintained a low profile. He sang on the début album by the veteran Jamaican saxophonist Andy Hamilton, contributing a version of Rodger's and Hart's 'You Are Too Beautiful'. He attended Barry White's concert in Milan and joined the superstar to duet on 'Let The Music Play'. In the summer of 1990 he drove across the Alps from Milan to Montreux on the banks of Lake Geneva for the town's world famous jazz festival. He had met Miles Davis before and regarded him as a friend. Their time together in Montreux was to be their last. "I met him there with Quincy Jones, and he was actually in very, very good spirits, he was really enjoying it. I'm not a particularly cosmic person, but Miles was a magician. Miles Davis was not of this earth. If there is some kind of spiritual after-life I can assure you that Miles Davis is there. I don't think there's any question about that," he said.

The premature death of Davis robbed Hucknall of a chance to work with his idol. Talks had taken place between Hucknall and Davis' producer, Tommy LiPulma, and they were on the verge of setting a date for recording. Davis had told Hucknall that he was a fan of the group, reportedly proclaiming, 'I love that album, 'Picture Book', man!'

During the tour for 'A New Flame' the band's entourage had grown so that Hucknall lived a cosseted life. There was staff to wake him in the morning and others to cater for his every whim. It was an unreal environment and he was happy to escape it. "It's a situation in which the world revolves around you, and everyone comes to you as you sit on your little throne. It was such an eye-opener for me when I stopped working and started to get in touch with my old friends. Suddenly I had to start dealing with life on their terms. They'd be the ones saying, 'Sorry, can't make it; I've got to work'. At first your reaction is non-comprehension: 'What do you mean, you can't come to see me?' That's a great experience for someone like me. Suddenly your pop star ego gets a good slap on the face," he said.

The year's break allowed Hucknall to enjoy his wealth. There were unconfirmed rumours of clandestine investment in property but much of his spending was on travelling costs. Like many pop stars before him, he was able to travel the globe at will and as he had started relatively late he vowed to make up for lost time. "I could just lie in bed, yawning, and think: 'Where should I go today? Brazil? Yeah, that sounds nice...' And off I'd go and do that. In fact, I lived like that for a whole year, moving around as and when I felt like it. I've really got the travelling bug. If I'm anywhere for more than two or three weeks I get bored and move on. And that's exacerbated by the fact that I'm in a position where I don't have to stick at anything if I don't want to. After all, what's the point? If you're not enjoying yourself when you're not working, you're in big trouble," he told *Vox*.

His movements were trailed by the popular press and he was again photographed in the company of attractive women. Of the more famous faces by his side, there was singer Kim Wilde but more regularly the German tennis champion Steffi Graf. It was apparent that they had formed a close relationship although he scoffed at the notion that they were lovers. "We are good friends and I like watching her play tennis but that's it. I went to Germany recently and picked up a paper with a big picture of me and the headline, 'This is the man who loves Steffi'. It was hilarious," he said.

Steffi attended several Simply Red performances during the tour for 'A New Flame' and was given a special seat by the mixing desk. Hucknall elaborated on the 'just good friends' line by confiding to journalists that they were 'dear friends'. In an interview with Gill Pringle of the *Sunday Express* he used the term 'relationship' when speaking of the liaison with the tennis player.

The friendship between Hucknall and Graf was typical. Pop stars and sports stars had much in common - fame, adulation, wealth, youth, ambition, constant travel and a sense of isolation. In dating women like Brigitte Nielsen, Kim Wilde and Steffi Graf he was with kindred spirits. They were part of the same spurious goldfish bowl world encircled by the paparazzi with their tape recorders and cameras.

Hucknall, after a four-year apprenticeship, had adapted to fame and wealth. He scoffed at his earlier follies: "It was just excess, you took everything in excess. I saw another group doing the same thing and it was so funny - I saw so much of myself in these guys. They were at a record company dinner in Verona and their faces were just gleaming. They'd just had two hits in England. Somebody says, 'You want some more wine?' Yeah, yeah, yeah! 'More food?' Yeah! 'More girls, anything?' Yeah! In the first couple of years you just want it all, y'know," he told *The Guardian*.

If the welcome by the popular press was prickly, the quality papers offered scant respite. He was becoming a phenomenon and they wanted to prod his psyche. They discovered that he lacked the etiquette of wealth. The accent was slovenly and he mis-pronounced vowel sounds. He was tacky (the ruby in the tooth, for instance), he was cocksure, his records appealed predominantly to the working class!

Unlike scores of pop performers drawn from the same class, he refused to be patronised or intimidated by snobbery and

'I could just lie in bed, yawning, and think: Where should I go today? Brazil? Yeah, that sounds nice...'

this, more than the minor style points picked off by condescending journalists, contributed to the stereo-typing of himself as arrogant and truculent. "I think his image in the press is a lot to do with the way he reacts to journalists who I think he sees as being a bit prescriptive in telling him how he ought to behave and imposing a moral code, an *NME*-type of moral code, and that's the sort of thing that makes him rebel," said *Arena*'s Mark Cooper.

Before rehearsals for the next album, Hucknall had to find a new rhythm section. The Japanese drummer Gota Yashiki took up the vacant stool and Shaun Ward joined on bass. Ward had previously played with the relatively unknown UK group, Everyday People, but was widely respected as a brilliant musician and promising songwriter. He had spent many years in the Sheffield band Floy Joy and was 31 when he joined Simply Red.

Gota was the son of a classical percussionist from Kyoto, Japan. He had played in Japanese bands Plastic, Melon and Mute Beat before moving to London in 1988 to work as a drum programmer. Before joining Simply Red he had programmed the drums for Soul II Soul.

Stewart Levine had again influenced the choice, he had introduced Gota to Simply Red. He was 29-years-old and brought the group a multi-national touch. Hucknall liked the image: "We're a peace keeping force for the UN. We travel around the world and make peace," he joked.

Stewart Levine's tight but warm production on 'A New Flame' had re-invigorated the sound and there was no need to change the formula for the next record. "I trust and completely believe in Mick's relationship with Stewart Levine," said Rashman.

At the end of 1990 Rashman had to re-negotiate the contract with East West (WEA had changed its trading name in the UK) and secured an advance of £1 million for the forthcoming album. Simply Red booked into Condulmer studio, housed in a 16th Century villa on the outskirts of Venice in northern Italy.

'We're a peace keeping force for the UN. We travel around the world and make peace'.

Max Hole, managing director of East West and Hucknall's main A&R contact, was one of the first outside the group to hear the new songs. "You always have high hopes but sometimes records don't do as well as you'd hoped. I first heard 'Stars' in Venice before it was remixed and I was pretty guardedly optimistic," he said. Rashman was more forthcoming and described the moment when he first heard the tracks as the greatest of his life.

The first public airing of the new material came in September 1991 when 'Something Got Me Started' was released as a single. Co-written by Hucknall and McIntyre (described by Hucknall as his 'deputy sheriff'), it was an excellent opening - fresh, light, strident and catchy.

It reached number 11 in the UK charts and was followed two weeks later, on September 30, by the album 'Stars', a collection of top-notch pop songs bound in an atmosphere of effortless confidence. It was about to make Simply Red's career up until this point appear small-time, such was the incredible reaction.

'Something Got Me Started', the album's opener, was followed by the title track, an enchanting ballad sung in a deep, husky voice with keyboards and under-stated guitar lines complementing the celestial feel. The song worked, like most of the others on the record, because of its relaxed air. This was a band entering a new level of maturity without the need to stamp its feet and reinforce every musical nuance with needless instrumentation.

'Thrill Me' had a carefree feel, swaying rhythmically to the textures created by the brass drive of Ian Kirkham and Tim Kellett's keyboard punctuation. The first overtly political lyrical reference was in 'Your Mirror'. In classic rock 'n' roll (bad) grammar, Hucknall claimed that society, 'don't care about nobody else': the tune was better than the prose as it stuttered in the fashion of 'A New Flame' before breaking into a gushing, warm chorus.

Gota played a beat influenced by Hip-Hop on 'She's Got It Bad' but the music on top was slick, laidback funk. The chorus was not as honed as the others and the vocal yelps and tricky instrumental passages failed to shape this most disappointing song in the set.

The band were back on top form with 'For Your Babies', a song of beautiful simplicity. An acoustic guitar lick led the way to a seductive croon before the soulful chords were shared equally between the guitar and keyboard.

Bob Marley's 'Jamming' was clearly a reference point for 'Model'. It featured a chugging off-beat guitar along with a plethora of traditional reggae sounds - a deep bass, smooth guitar lines, loose and spartan drum beat. It raised itself above parody through another strong chorus.

'How Could I Fall' allowed the band to indulge themselves without losing sight of the main force of the song. Kirkham brought a winning rough edge to the jazz smoothness with rasping saxophone runs.

The vague experimental slant continued on 'Freedom'. Rowetta, a singer who had previously worked with Manchester band Happy Mondays, added to the spiritual feel with her powerful range. It was a clever shift from the traditional pop song format.

'Wonderland' was a direct and frank attack on Margaret Thatcher and policies Hucknall claimed had taken Britain into the massive slump of the late 1980s and early 1990s. The music was sweet and mesmeric but the message was couched in sarcasm. He sang earnestly of a Wonderland where everything was beautiful except its people were crippled by debt. It was a bleak vision of a depressed UK where the future was unclear and avarice thrived. It was purposely chosen to close the album and provide food for thought.

Apart from the obvious commitment to strong songs, the record provided the group with a strong organic aura. Stewart Levine and Hucknall (he was credited as co-producer) had engineered a sound that embraced pop with a fair degree of ambience.

The marketing of the record was meticulously organised by East West, and in line with company policy it was undertaken wholly in the artist's country of origin, the UK. There was a willingness to devote finance and manpower to the project because, in the middle of a worldwide recession, this was one record guaranteed to bring in plenty of revenue.

Hucknall had presented East West with a set of songs that lent itself to imaginative marketing. "This was a recession-buster. We always thought it was a great record, really from the get-go. And really, from the beginning, it sold huge quantities. We thought it was even stronger than 'A New Flame'. We all knew we had a winning album," said the group's press officer, Lee Ellen Newman.

The brief had been to capture pacific, magical imagery and package the album around it. The pose for the sleeve was set up by the art director/photographer Zanna and was a pastiche of a famous photograph from Hollywood's silent era with Hucknall taking the place of Mary Pickford. "The photo was absolutely gorgeous and it was clear it was a wonderful image to brand, which is marketing a range of products from the same artist," said Elyse Taylor, marketing head of East West.

The sleeve showed Hucknall bowed down as if in prayer as the clouds and sky moved around him. The colours were mainly dark shades of blue, it was a contrast to the harsh primary colours on earlier album sleeves. The 'sky' on the photograph was added afterwards and was actually a mixture of colours created at dawn and nightfall. On the other photographs on the album Hucknall was swathed in a patterned sack-cloth, his hair loose, tumbling gently to his shoulders. The message was clear - it was an airy, wistful record with the high quota of top quality tunes expected from a maturing songwriter.

Critics sensed that Hucknall had exceeded expectations and the mainstream reviews for 'Stars' were favourable: 'The sheer class of much of this record is to be admired' - *Daily Mail*; 'Old Red has finally made an album as good as he says it is. 'Stars' keeps shining' - *The Guardian*; 'Another meticulously-produced catalogue of blue-eyed soul songs' - *The Times*; 'Really rather good' - *Q*.

The UK weekly music press, now shrunk to just two papers, the *NME* and *Melody Maker*, and separated only by a flight of stairs in the same building, was still unwilling to embrace Hucknall. *Melody Maker* dubbed 'Stars', 'a Christmas present for gran' and *NME* said it was, 'an exercise in no-style over no-content.' Hucknall, to them, was making grown-up music that wiped its feet by the stereo. It was polite, ordered, and blended in with the black lampshade from Habitat.

'Old Red has finally made an album as good as he says it is...'

"In the end, the punters made the decision and went for the record that gave them the largest all-round listening value and pleasure. With Simply Red people expect jazz, funk, soul, blues, reggae and ballads - that's good." Elliot Rashman was distilling the reasons why 'Stars' was fast becoming one of the most successful albums ever released and would eventually become the best-selling CD of all time in the UK.

At East West Records Max Hole had his own theory. "There are two reasons. Firstly, this hasn't happened overnight. Simply Red have built up a solid fan base. They are one of the few groups that people will buy an album without hearing it, because Simply Red are equated with quality. Secondly, Mick Hucknall is a great singer, the best of his generation, black or white. He can sing an average song and make it great; with great songs you've got a clear winner. Suddenly Simply Red are acceptable to everyone."

A year after its release 'Stars' had sold almost seven million copies throughout the world, 2.4 million in the UK alone. By April 1993 it had sold eight million copies worldwide. Despite being released late in the year it was the best-selling album of 1991 and matched the feat in 1992 - only Dire Straits' 'Brothers In Arms' had done the same.

It spent 47 weeks in the UK Top 10, rarely dropping out of the Top Five. On the run-in to Christmas 1991 it sold an average of 100,000 copies a week. In the first year it regained the top position on five separate occasions - only Simon and Garfunkel's 'Bridge Over Troubled Water' LP had done the same.

Sales of 'A New Flame' increased and just a month after the release of 'Stars' its predecessor notched up its six millionth sale, meaning, in September 1992, that Simply Red had sold 20 million albums in their career. The figures were made additionally impressive considering their relatively weak profile in the US (13 per cent

The New European

'He can sing an average song and make it great; with great songs you've got a clear winner...'

of total sales). It gave an indication of their saturation in other territories, especially Europe.

In April 1992 Hucknall was chosen as songwriter of the year at the Ivor Novello awards ceremony - the critical acclaim appeared to be mirroring the commercial success.

During the countdown to the release of 'Stars' there were fears that the timing might have been askew. Although late-

'I don't want to be a bitch, but outselling Prince isn't difficult…'

September was traditionally the time of high sales with Christmas looming, it coincided with a heavy release schedule. Michael Jackson, U2 and Dire Straits released new albums at the same time and sales were still heavy for previous releases from Guns N' Roses, Queen, Genesis, Tina Turner, Prince and Eurythmics.

In the event, 'Stars' easily out-sold the rest in the UK. The Eurythmics' greatest hits album almost pipped 'Stars' as the best-seller of 1991 but after the final week the figures showed 'Stars' had sold 300,000 more - and Eurythmics had enjoyed seven more months of sales than Simply Red.

The sales battle intrigued Hucknall, it appealed to his fiercely competitive nature. He had little sympathy for the performers below him in the sales league. On Prince: "I don't want to be a bitch, but outselling Prince isn't difficult. If people knew what his album sales were they would be amazed. He doesn't have big album sales." On Dire Straits: "I have no sympathy with Dire Straits. If they're going to release a single like 'Calling Elvis' with the way things are at the moment, I criticise them for it." On Genesis: "Who needs another Genesis album at this point in time? Phil's not even been away. When is he going to go away?"

He mustered some sympathy for Tina Turner whose greatest hits album was kept off the top spot by 'Stars'. "I happen to have a soft spot for Tina Turner, not just the music, but her whole story. And I love seeing her do well. And when she couldn't get to the number one spot because of us, well, I felt really guilty. I felt like a louse. I had a real problem with that - I really like Tina."

The year's break had energised Hucknall and he was ready to undertake a hectic promotional campaign and tour. In readiness for the endless rounds of shows, interviews, late nights and hotels he took up a strict fitness régime. He jogged several miles each day and monitored his eating. He lost more weight, slimming down from 14 to 12 stones. He cut down his alcohol intake, limiting himself to the occasional glass of wine. He had been warned by doctors that alcohol was linked to the skin complaint eczema of which he had a mild condition.

On his return to the public eye, observers were surprised to find a lean, radiant Hucknall, happy to sip mineral water and bound around in sandals and a track suit. His hair was different too - still red, of course, but longer and shaped into tight thin spirals. The dreadlocks were woven every three months and washed in mineral water.

He had lost none of the confidence, indeed much of it was now justified. "It's been a long time since we made a record but there doesn't seem to be anything that's taken our place. I don't feel there's people out there doing what we're doing, which is nice. I don't see anyone around who's getting near me. I don't want that to sound arrogant because if someone's a great singer, I'm happy to acknowledge that. If somebody's great then, hey, I'm there, but I don't really know of anyone," he said.

There was a paradox; the singer who had started out with a song called 'Money's Too Tight (To Mention)' had become, seven years later, a multi-millionaire. In July 1992 it was speculated that he had a personal fortune of £15 million. Money was no longer tight and it meant he could own two homes and a red Mazda sports car worth a reported £30,000.

It was noticed that 'Stars' did not contain a cover version. Critics saw the move as bold, Hucknall without a safety net. It had been a deliberate policy, he was concerned that he was still perceived as an artist who had greater success with other people's material. He was determined to establish himself as a songwriter on his own terms.

In interviews Hucknall expanded on the subjects covered in the lyrics of the album tracks. 'Wonderland' saw Hucknall on his soapbox. "Margaret Thatcher sold us down the river. She absolutely sold us off. 'Wonderland' is about discovering that we're in much the same position as we were when Margaret Thatcher came to power - and many are actually worse off, even though they were part of the Thatcher dream. At the moment England is in a state of shell shock. The country doesn't know what's hit it," he told *The People* magazine.

He considered 'For Your Babies', written during the Gulf War, to be his best ever song. It was penned after he had seen many of his friends, including Rashman, have children as they moved through their thirties. "It's just weird to see somebody giving a piece of their life away for the first time. A part of them has come to life and at the same time they've sacrificed a piece of their lives just by having a kid. It's just wild seeing the change in people," he said.

Fans agreed that 'For Your Babies' was the best track on 'Stars'. A poll was held in the band's official fanzine *Open Up The Red Box* and it received 31 per cent of the votes. The other popular tracks were 'Stars' with 18 per cent and 'Thrill Me' with 15 per cent.

The lives of Simply Red's fans were mirroring Hucknall's own; anyone who had bought 'Picture Book' as a 21-year-old was now approaching 30 and doubtlessly many were having children of their own or seeing their friends have them.

The album hardly needed another hit single to consolidate sales but the title track 'Stars' reached number eight in November 1991 and gave the band a good showing in the important Christmas charts. The video, shot in California's sun-scorched Mojave Desert, again captured the terrestrial tones and hues of the album packaging.

East West noticed that the band's fan base was roughly categorised as 21-years-old and upwards. In an attempt to attract younger fans and appeal to the demanding club audience, two of the freshest mixing talents were asked to alter the dial settings on the single 'Stars'. Steve 'Silk' Hurley and P.M. Dawn were happy to re-direct the band towards the dance floor by adding the necessary rhythmical strength to the song with re-mixes on the 12" and CD versions.

Hucknall allowed the film cameras from TV AM to trail him for a special three-part documentary screened in the UK on November 26, 27 and 28, 1991. The shooting took place during a promotional tour to Rome and the short interviews were interspersed with videos of the band's best known songs.

Hucknall scanned the countries on all sides of his Milan base and declared himself a federalist. He visited a, 'Tom Waits sort of a guy' in Los Angeles who etched the European flag on to his right arm. Each star on it represented a country which was part of the European alliance. The album's title was chosen partly to reflect a pro-European stance. "I feel very European. I'm a supporter of us being a unified state, or a place where we work together economically but keep our own individuality as a country," he said.

There were more reasons why 'Stars' had been the title. He had spent many nights on beaches around the globe staring up at the skies and he was entranced by their heavenly quality. On visits to Manchester he had met emerging performers from the city who were experiencing their first sample of stardom. He had a quiet, knowing chuckle as he saw them beginning a process he had already transcended. Again, it was an influence on the choice of title.

It was clear during the round of promotional interviews that both Hucknall and Rashman relished the image of European Men. "Britain's finished. As far as I can see, it's had it. Compared to us, the Italians are so civilised. They think of us as Third World. They say, 'Poor Britain, poor Britain," Rashman cooed to Q.

Hucknall continued the theme: "It might sound dreadfully unpatriotic but there's not a lot I miss about England. I lived in England for 25 years and now I'm wreaking my revenge." As if to consolidate their view of undeveloped Britain, they declined to drink the tap water, preferring instead to swig from bottles of Evian water.

The haughtiness was compounded by a plague of name-dropping to the man from Q magazine, John Naughton. Hucknall called professional footballers by their nicknames and sent them tickets to attend his shows. He spent weekends in Paris with Sean Penn. He was an acquaintance of Jack Nicholson. And for how long had words like 'dreadfully' been part of his vocabulary?

The article irritated Hucknall because, he claimed, it contained little reference to music. "Everybody else in the same issue talks about music except Mick, so, if one were to think seriously about that, one might come away and think that Mick is the equivalent of a Page Three bimbo," said his publicist, Lee Ellen Newman.

Hucknall was in the later stages of pop ascendancy: a friend of the stars, stylish, travelled, culture-hungry and articulate. The transformation from brat to sophisticate was complete. Unlike other pop icons he was showing no appetite for over-indulgence. He was perhaps the archetype of the modern pop saint, sipping only the elixir of music and moderation as his bank balance bulged.

"I've heard he's a really nice bloke these days, quite charming and gentle. Obviously all the travelling and meeting people has made him more mature. When he was younger he was very temperamental. There was always something about him though. He had a kind of awe, I've only met a few people with that kind of quality a few times in my life," said Colin Sinclair, owner of Simply Red's first rehearsal base.

The packaging of the album and Hucknall's more relaxed demeanour contributed finally to a more wholesome media image in the UK. "I think he is being taken seriously now. He did have almost a caricature image before of someone who liked to date pretty women, and

'I feel very European. I'm a supporter of us being a unified state...'

quite a lot of them, and he liked to spend a lot of time in clubs. In the past year people have realised that he writes great songs and listens to a lot of music. He also has intelligent and thought-out opinions on a wide range of issues," said Lee Ellen Newman.

Everyone still wanted to know - why was the album so popular, Mick? "Well, it has the appearance of sounding clear and very simple but it's very complex. So simple and complex is a contradiction, but that's what it is. There's no waste on the record, no frills, no showing off. It's just great musicians making music. For me, 'Stars' is a really serious piece of shit, a fucking well-serious record that I believe will be seen as a timeless classic. I'm even still playing it over and over myself, which is unusual for me once a record is completed," he said.

The other explanation of its appeal, centred fanatically on the record's supposed socio-economic and political thrust, was more long-winded and pretension scented the air. "When I took a year out from 'A New Flame', a lot of things happened in the world and happened in Britain that were very, very inspiring. The Berlin Wall coming down, Saddam Hussein, and for English people, the rise and fall of Margaret Thatcher. I don't think people realised initially how much it really affected them as people, losing their matron, their nurse, the one that gave them their cod liver oil every day.

"I think that the album catches the mood of that sense of loss, particularly 'Wonderland' and, 'What the hell are we going to do now?' and there are a lot of things in it that I felt and I think a lot of other people felt at the same time. It's as if people have had enough of living this way now.

"When I left college, I'm not trying to say I'm some type of visionary, but at that particular time it struck me that as a society we were becoming very self-centred and very, very into just making bucks, just making money and just being encouraged by the government to spend and make money. This society was creating a desperation among people to hold on to their jobs; this tension, I was really upset about it. I think a lot of people are now thinking we needn't have these social problems if we lived in a different system than we're living now," he said in a radio interview with the BBC in 1992.

'Stars', despite Hucknall's claim, was not bought for its polemic rhetoric. It sold in quantity because it contained great tunes sung well by a favourite son. In fact, a survey conducted by East West revealed that many people liked Hucknall because, 'He seems like one of us' - in other words, a pop Everyman.

He still issued fundamental Socialist themes - education for all, better training, equality, care for the young, sick, and old, greater freedom - and he was prepared to take on the mantle as quasi-spokesman, despite criticising pop performers like Bono for doing the same.

He was seen as a figure more synonymous with Conservative traits than Labour. The ferocious ambition, the single-mindedness, the acquisition of wealth, the independence: he was, unwittingly, an offspring of the Thatcher generation. He argued that he came from a previous age, when caring and sharing still mattered. "If I was 18 now, I don't think I'd be able to go to polytechnic, and I don't think I would have become the person I am, who became Simply Red, without that privilege. When I was going to college you got a grant, but now you have to pay it back. It's back to where middle class and upper middle class kids get an education and a lot of the lower class ones don't," he said.

Thankfully, Hucknall's self-mocking humour was still by his side. There was enough evidence to show he was over-earnest

'I'm not white enough for a lot of stations because I sound too black'.

many more times than he was pious. "'Wonderland' is a song that makes the point that after 12 years of Thatcher there's only a tiny minority of rich bastards like me who can honestly say they're better off. Which does leave me rather embarrassed actually," he told *The Sunday Times*.

Simply Red were part of the backdrop to British life. Their music was piped through speakers in shopping precincts and at any moment it was possible to flick across the dial of a radio and find one of their songs being played. In towns and cities posters advertising their records and concerts were invariably being put up or taken down. The saturation was intense. The nation - hairdressers, footballers, shopkeepers, factory workers and schoolteachers - were singing along with Hucknall.

It had been a slog, 13 years since The Frantic Elevators released their first record and eight years since Simply Red's début. Hucknall was determined that the history was noted.

"I'd say it's popular listening. I strike a chord. I honestly don't think this album should be gotten out of perspective compared to the other ones. Before we released this album we were one of Britain's most successful bands. All we are now is Britain's most successful band," he said.

Despite the supposed indifference to greater success in the US, it was obviously still on the agenda - it would be remiss of any pop management and record company to overlook such a lucrative market and it was also a challenge Hucknall could not resist. "It's not a problem with the record company or anything like that, it's a social issue. It's about the fact that America is a segregated society, and we are a very together band. The music we make is black, white, yellow and all kinds of colours. What happens over there is that I'm not black enough to get played on the black radio stations because they've got to take care of their own artists, since white radio doesn't, and I'm not white enough for a lot of stations because I sound too black," he said.

Some critics suggested that the US did not have a 'need' for Simply Red. Unlike Europe which, broadly speaking, did not have a well-spring of black talent to draw upon, America's musical culture was steeped in a long tradition of black artists.

In April, 1988, Hucknall had chosen his top 10 favourite records on Radio One. It included songs by Marvin Gaye, Billie Holiday, Keith Rowe, Otis Redding, Gladys Knight, James Brown, Ella Fitzgerald, Miles Davis, Augustus Pablo and Aretha Franklin. They were all black and, apart from one, American. Why, therefore, should Americans buy Simply Red records when they already had the raw material from where Hucknall - a white Englishman - had mined his inspiration?

chapter 9

Like Frank Sinatra

Unlike many artists with a recording contract of strict deadlines, Simply Red were granted freedom to move at their own pace. Hucknall said he was in no rush to follow-up 'Stars' - even mentioning that a five year gap was not out of consideration. "I'm really not under any great pressure to make music. If I don't have a record, I don't record, it doesn't come out. I'm not under any pressure, contractually or anything, to make albums within any given period of time. I'm signed for a quantity of albums that can be recorded at my leisure. I don't need to make another album for 10 years and they can't do a thing about it, so that kind of pressure is out," he told Ireland's Hot Press.

The single 'For Your Babies' released in January 1992 supplied the press with a new angle. 'Mick Longs To Be Simply Wed' said the *Daily Mirror*. The song, a plaintive ballad with a faintly nostalgic air, begged the question: 'Did Mick Hucknall himself want a baby?'. And, to their surprise, he said, 'Yes, he probably did'. The band were at the beginning of a mammoth tour due to end more than a year later in April 1993 and Hucknall admitted that his fast world had not, so far, had room for a relationship - and, of course, children.

"To have a steady partner you need time to develop a relationship, and that comes about through settling in an area for a given period of time. When I have a more regular lifestyle, I feel that's when something like a proper relationship, and even children, could happen," he told the *Mirror*.

The 'freelance love machine' had come of age. After 'A New Flame' he had spent his time off in peripatetic fashion but this time he wanted to find Mrs Right. "I hate the formula of a submissive wife, rose garden and snotty kids. I've no preconceptions about it, I just know that I want some kids at some point, because I like kids. I find pregnant women very sexy. I don't know why, I guess I'm kind of weird," he told *Vox* in March 1992.

'I find pregnant women very sexy. I don't know why, I guess I'm kind of weird'.

Above:
Hucknall with model
Christina Kumlin.

Below:
Laughing with Christina.

There was speculation that he wanted to foster a flourishing relationship with the Swedish model, Christina Kumlin. "We met at a party three years ago and have stayed friends ever since. He's my best friend in the whole world. We have a very strong relationship - very close," said the 19-year-old to the *News of the World*.

On their exhaustive tour Simply Red played 127 concerts in 1992 to 2.75 million people in four continents. Several on-the-road clichés were challenged. Women were appointed to senior positions in the road crew. Sophie Ridley was made tour manager, Clare Grady, assistant tour manager and Yvonne Melville wardrobe mistress. The management team was also composed predominantly of women with Lindy Everton, Soozii Walker and Andrea Irvine helping Bob Harding administer the concerts.

It had a tangible effect on the mood of the tour. "We just found that a lot of the macho bullshit gets cut out. It wasn't anything planned or whatever, it just happened that more and more women joined the crew, and suddenly everyone began to be more considerate to each other. If someone was having trouble at home everyone knew about it, and we were all being extra nice to the guy. It really changed the atmosphere and made it more like a family," said Hucknall.

The tour started in January 1992 in Dublin before moving to the UK and mainland Europe for three months. Another single was released from 'Stars' in April 1992, the sassy 'Thrill Me'. It presented once more the band's upbeat, dance-driven side.

On Easter Sunday a concert performance shot in Hamburg just a few weeks earlier was broadcast in the UK. The programme was produced by Granada Television and screened in most regions of the UK. It attracted four and a half million viewers. An incident involving the concert film indicated that Rashman had not lost his touchiness. A favour for a favour had been his policy since the beginning and it was not a flexible idiom. Granada's Bob Dickenson had earlier written an unflattering review of Simply Red's 'Men And Women' album for *City Life*. He thought no more of it.

He was explaining the film idea to Simply Red's plugger, Neil Ferris, when he sensed an atmosphere. He was then told unceremoniously, 'Under no circumstances would Simply Red go ahead with anything at Granada if it included the involvement of Bob Dickenson'.

At first Dickenson was mystified, he could hardly remember the review in *City Life*, indeed others sprang to mind, positive ones he had contributed to the *NME*, especially in the early days of the group. Ferris informed him that if he wrote an apologetic letter to Rashman he might be forgiven. Dickenson refused but assured him that his involvement beyond the early stages would be minimal anyway. Finally, legal staff at Granada had to draw up a document stating that Dickenson would play no part in the project.

After 10 shows in the US and Canada the band returned to the UK for five sell-out 'One Day Internationals' in July at London's Wembley Stadium (two shows), Manchester's Lancashire County Cricket ground (two shows) and the Gateshead International Stadium (one show). They appeared before 80,000 fans at Wembley on July 12 1992 - almost exactly seven years after the Live Aid concert.

The band had warmed up for the UK shows by appearing at the Montreux Jazz Festival where they had first played in 1986. The set of 26 songs was a mix of their own material and interpretations of old standards like Cole Porter's 'Love For Sale'. The festival's founder and director, Claude Nobs, had

long been a supporter of the band. "Simply Red has the uniqueness of blending classic pop, rhythm and blues, a touch of jazz, some timeless songs and Mick Hucknall's great writing on both melodies and lyrics; all a magnificent way to unite crowds from all musical persuasions," he said.

The relentless touring continued as Simply Red moved on to Eire, Israel, Greece, Australia, New Zealand, Singapore, Hong Kong and finally back to London in November 1992. Towards the end Hucknall was weary of the schedule: "I'm tired of travelling round the world, spending most of my life in airports and waking up in different hotel bedrooms. I want to start sleeping in the same bed every night. People don't realise that's the sort of thing you miss."

'Your Mirror' was released in July to capitalise on the popularity of the live shows which had sold out within hours of tickets going on sale. The record coincided with the news that 'Stars' had sold five million copies. 'Your Mirror' was another excellent pop/soul song and took Simply Red back into the UK Top 20.

Their singles were, for the first time in their career, consistently well-received. The huge fan base was enough to take any song they released into the Top 40 regardless of radio airplay. Another survey carried out by East West showed that most of their fans would buy a Simply Red record whether or not they had actually heard it first - it was proof of a rare devotion.

In confirmation of his popular vote, Hucknall was made the *Daily Star's* official 'King of Rock' in September 1992. Michael Jackson had started a furore when he asked radio and television presenters to refer to him as 'The King' in interviews during his world tour. The newspaper put it to the test and invited readers to vote for their king. Hucknall came out on top with almost 400 more votes than Bono of U2. Michael Jackson trailed in fifth place behind Hucknall, Bono, Prince and Bruce Springsteen.

Rashman claimed, humorously in the circumstances, that there was no orchestration behind Hucknall's rise to stardom. "There hasn't been a gameplan. Malcolm McLaren-style strategies turn out to be incredibly short-lived. There are no theories. Theories don't work. If there is a secret, it's being able to create the best possible conditions for Mick and the band to be creative," was Rashman's white lie.

Part of Hucknall's appeal lay in the public's perception of him as ordinary. Unlike Prince or Madonna, there was nothing other-worldly or cartoon-like about his personality, he had remained raw and unfettered. He drew heavily on a similar strand of blue-collar support that had propelled stars like Bruce Springsteen.

Whether Rashman, East West and Hucknall himself had been aware of his broad appeal and marketed him thus was open to question. There had been few grandiose artistic statements to challenge the common touch - no indulgent films, no major 're-invention' for each new record, no extravagant videos. It had all been more of a general rounding-off of his image rather than anything strikingly visible.

'I want to start sleeping in the same bed every night. People don't realise that's the sort of thing you miss'.

Rashman was keen to under-play the importance of Hucknall's marketing, it was part of a manager's job to do so. "Elliot has always got a very singular perspective on the music industry. 'Scheming' is the wrong word, but just sort of shrewd, thoughtful, sometimes off-beam in his pronouncements. There always seemed to be a strategy in his mind," said an insider.

In his new position as one of the world's most important performers, Hucknall spoke out during the autumn of 1992 about what he considered to be profiteering by the music business. "The amount of royalty we get compared to how much a CD is sold for is not justifiable in relation to the profit record companies make. They charge too much and it's not for the reason they give, that we're taking too much in royalties. That's just the biggest load of crap," he said.

He criticised the industry's plans to introduce two new formats, the digital compact cassette (DCC) and the minidisc, a miniature type of compact disc. He refused East West permission to release 'Stars' on DCC which was seen as the natural successor to the compact disc. "This is all a lid on a can of worms. It brings to light a whole series of questions on the morality and fairness of the music industry," he said in a radio interview.

Hucknall also questioned the traditional right of a record company to own master tapes of recorded songs when they were ultimately paid for by artists (record companies paid the artist an 'advance' to cover studio hire but this money was later reclaimed by the company from sales). "When I walk out of that room they own the tape. I wrote them, I sat there with an acoustic guitar and wrote them. How can anyone say that they own that piece of me?" he asked.

Elliot Rashman was also keen to have his say. He was widely quoted in the trade press, speaking out, he claimed, on behalf of artists and fans. He joined forces with Ed Bicknell, manager of Dire Straits, to form the International Managers' Forum and lobby record companies. Rashman persuaded the Manchester Labour MP, Gerald Kaufman, to make representations to Parliament about the deliberate over-pricing of CDs in the UK.

Rashman had earlier adopted a fairly low profile but he showed a new willingness to share the spotlight He, like Hucknall, had moved to the top of his profession and he was enamoured of the view. In the summer of 1992 he helped organise 'In The City', a special music business seminar held in Manchester. He assembled a managers' panel and was delighted when the legendary Peter Grant, formerly Led Zeppelin's manager, attended.

In October with Christmas in mind, East West released a live concert video called 'A Starry Night'. The video was a joint production with Granada Television and was basically a re-packaging of the programme the station had aired six months earlier. It was filmed at a concert at the Sport Halle stadium in Hamburg and also featured backstage interviews with Hucknall and the band.

Two hundred members of Simply Red's fan club had been allowed access to the two-hour soundcheck during the afternoon of the show and the band lined-up for photographs for them. The video was well shot and managed to catch a fair degree of intimacy considering the vastness of the concert arena.

A month after the video and again a tactical move to boost the group's end-of-year profile, an EP was released. The 'Montreux EP' contained four songs recorded in the summer at the jazz festival. 'Let's welcome Simply Red' ran the spoken introduction before Hucknall, unaccompanied save for an over-enthusiastic audience, sang the Cole Porter classic, 'Love For Sale'. Fritz McIntyre on piano backed the expressive voice on 'Drowning In My Own Tears', a Henry Glover song best known for the version recorded by Ray Charles. The third cover was an old live favourite, Bill Withers' 'Granma's Hands'. The only original track was 'Lady Godiva's Room', which although five years old, had the lilting melody of most of the songs on 'Stars'. The EP in record company terms was effectively a holding operation. It put the band back into the minds of the public just in time for Christmas. The choice of tracks and the style of delivery was important, however, because it helped assuage the notion that Simply Red were merely a pop hit machine.

East West continued its policy of aggressively marketing 'Stars' and funded a major television advertising campaign during Christmas 1992. The stylish adverts were broadcast more than 150 times over three weeks at a cost of £300,000. Newspaper adverts in the local and national press were run simultaneously.

The basic line-up was augmented by backing vocalists, Dee Johnson and Myllenda Lay who had previously sung with UB40 and Robert Palmer. It was planned to have just one backing singer but after hearing them sing together Hucknall asked them both to appear with the group. The only other slight alteration was that Kellett concentrated increasingly on keyboards rather than the trumpet.

'I wrote them, I sat there with an acoustic guitar and wrote them. How can anyone say that they own that piece of me?'

The 'Stars' Simply Red line-up (from left) Gota, Tim Kellett, Fritz McIntyre, Hucknall, Shaun Ward, Tan Kirkham and Heitor T.P.

The touring party had grown considerably over the years and as well as the group itself there were now two backing singers; a personal assistant to Hucknall (Paul Dallanegra); stage manager (Pip Betteridge); three instrument technicians (Rab Randall, Merv Pearson and Ray Walters); six truck drivers; six lighting technicians; five bus drivers; four caterers; three carpenters; three designers; three sound technicians; two merchandisers; two riggers; and numerous other assistants. In total the crew amounted to 41 people, costing more than £150,000 to keep on the road per week of the tour.

As widely expected, the band's achievements were recognised at the Brit Awards in February 1993. They received an award for being best group and Hucknall was voted best male artist. He was presented with his award by Lisa Stansfield, another performer noted for her strong voice and soul-based pop, born just 15 miles from Denton in Rochdale. Hucknall and McIntyre entertained the members of the British Phonographic Industry with a version of 'Wonderland'.

After the ceremony Hucknall held a press conference and announced that he was forming a production company to scout for new talent. Dreams, run by Hucknall and Gota, invited young musicians to send in demo tapes. Hucknall promised that he would work in the studio with artists he found particularly exciting.

There were no plans for Hucknall to appear live or on record with Simply Red during 1993 but guitarist Heitor TP spent the spring working on a solo album for East West on which there was a possibility Hucknall might sing. An insider revealed that Simply Red would record another album, 'When they were ready' but hinted that it could be in the autumn of 1994, three years on from 'Stars'.

It was noticed during the spring of 1993 that Hucknall's physique was no longer merely trim. He had lost more weight so that his face appeared gaunt and thin. The features that had floated on a round face were now piercing and strong against the hard geometric lines of his cheeks and jawbone. The untidy beard, pulled to a point on his sharp chin, made him appear older than his real age.

Journalists who had earlier mocked his rounded figure began speculating. *The Sunday News and Echo*, a sensationalist tabloid based in Manchester, suggested that there was perhaps cause for concern. "They're kidding! I think he looks fantastic. He looks great, he exercises a lot. No, he's in good shape. I guess you have to find an angle and that's the burden of the journalist, finding something new to say," said the band's press officer, Lee Ellen Newman.

Two unauthorised biographies on Hucknall were published in April 1993, 'Red Mick' by Mick Middles and 'Simply Mick' by father and son team, Robin and Rob McGibbon. Both were serious works, the latter anecdotal and concentrating largely on his pre-Simply Red days. Neither received co-operation from So What and were written without Hucknall's consent.

The huge demand in their home country meant that the original plan to play a handful of dates in November had to be developed into a full 23-date tour ending on December 20. Every ticket for the shows was sold within three days of going on sale. The stage set was completely re-arranged for the shows which included six dates at both the Birmingham NEC and Wembley Arena. It was a punishing schedule and some of the dates had to be pulled when Hucknall was struck down with a throat infection. The shows were immediately re-arranged for early in 1993.

BEST
GROUP

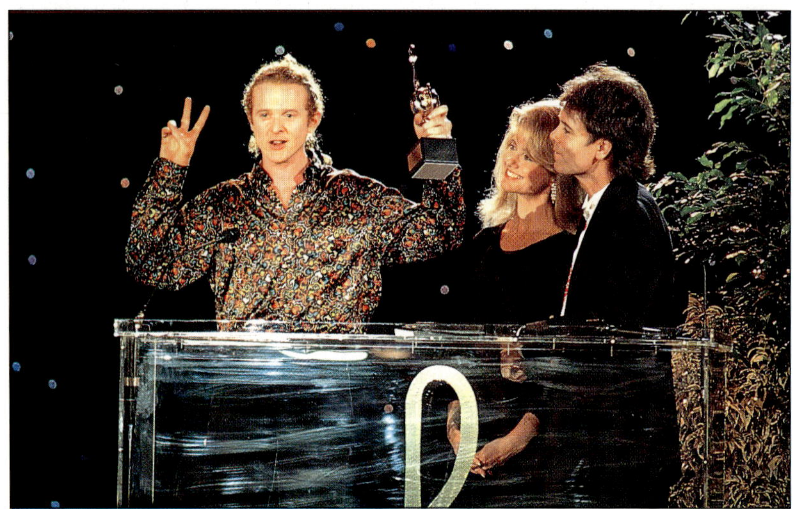

While vowing to continue his professional life until he could no longer physically sing ("I'm going to do a Frank Sinatra and go on forever"), Hucknall appeared during 1993 to be considering a new personal odyssey. "You only live once and I want a private life now. The kind of material things that I've got now, they're mine, they belong to me and I'm not going to give them away. But they don't change my life. I'm much more interested in personal happiness and being with people who know how to enjoy life," he told *Arena*.

'Stars' had effectively taken Hucknall to the apex of pop. The record was quickly viewed in the same light as, for instance, Pink Floyd's 'Dark Side Of The Moon' or Dire Straits' 'Brothers In Arms' - a commercial and critical masterpiece that occurred singularly during a performer's creative life span.

Above:
Hucknall with another award, watched by Cliff Richard.

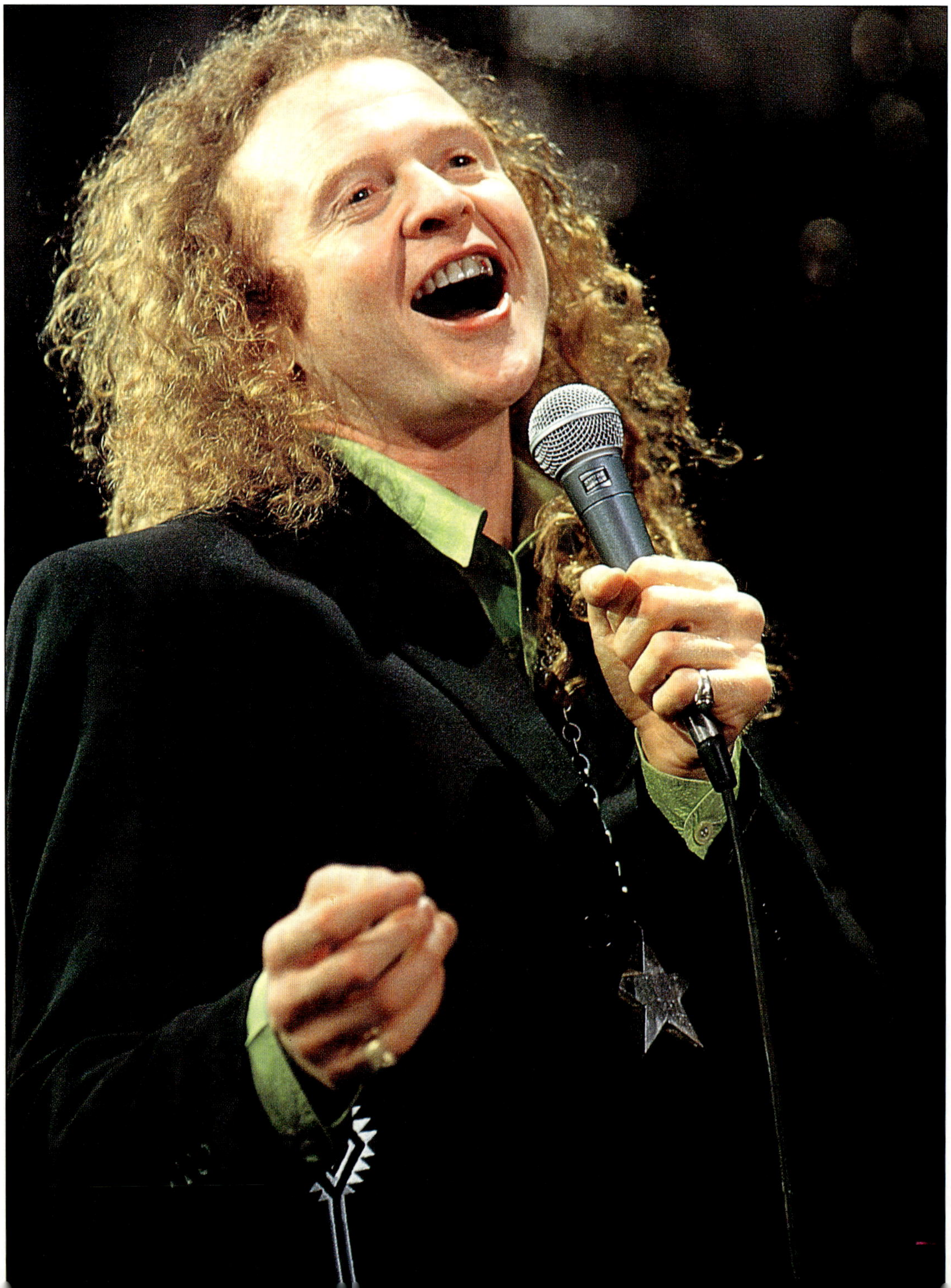

Other records indubitably held more cultural significance and contained, by turns, greater literacy, character, originality and energy but 'Stars' had a sprinkle of all these qualities coupled with superlative melodies. Although it drew from possibly conflicting forms of music, it was the perfect pop album, an opinion evidently shared by the listeners of Radio One who voted it the best ever rock album in a poll conducted over the May Day Bank Holiday of 1993. In second place was 'Sergeant Pepper's Lonely Hearts Club Band'.

Even musicians left by the wayside, ousted from Hucknall's and Rashman's gameplan, conceded that it was a fantastic album, some of them even conceding that their own influence might have watered down the mixture. "I think it is an amazing record, the tunes are just so strong. I think it is almost McCartneyesque," said Sylvan Richardson.

'Stars' was a rough stone of influences and ideas shaped into a smooth outline for popular consumption. It had been almost 16 years in the making - since Hucknall first picked up an acoustic guitar and coaxed his fingers into rudimentary chords and strummed out a basic accompaniment to his home-made tunes.

The 16 year journey had often been made against a backdrop of agitation. Sacked musicians, allegedly double-crossed and victims of double-speak, snapped at his heels and (they hoped) his conscience. They were joined by the critics, mocking and braying, intoxicated by the notion that Hucknall was a phoney, or a plagiarist, or a plebeian.

Perhaps he was disliked by UK critics because he was perceived as highly un-British: he was successful and flaunted it. They had made his name and music by-words for a safe, affluent and homogeneous lifestyle. It was a paradox that the foundation of his success was the gritty sensibility of rehearsal, dedication, musicianship, single-mindedness. In short, he should have been more of a focus of celebration than he actually was.

As for the musicians, deceived they claim, by the sleight of a phrase (what is a 'band' anyway?), only they could purge themselves of any lingering bitterness. Hucknall and Rashman *had* been ruthless and resorted to duplicity but 10 minutes in their company was enough - they were Simply Red, anyone else was a moth at the window.

"I think Mick's success kind of justifies all the crap that I went through in bands, driving to Birmingham to play to 15 people. It kind of justifies it that out of my contemporaries, someone has achieved all that. It wasn't me, but at least it shows that it can be done."

These were the words of a punk guitarist, now in his mid-thirties and selling fruit and vegetables to greengrocer shops. He walked the same Denton streets as Hucknall and shared the same stages at the beginning of his career. He sometimes hums along with Simply Red while driving the van.

'I'm going to do a Frank Sinatra and go on forever'.

discography

THE FRANTIC ELEVATORS

SINGLES

Voice In The Dark/Passion/Every Day I Die
TJM Records TJM 5 (7") June 1979

You Know What You Told Me/
Production Prevention
Erics Records ERICS 006 (7")
December 1980

Searching For The Only One/Hunchback
Of Notre Dame
Crackin' Up Records CRAK 1 (7")
July 1981

Holding Back The Years/Pistols In My Brain
No Waiting Records WAT 1 (7") October 1982

ALBUMS

THE EARLY YEARS LP
Voice in the Dark/EveryDayI Die/Passion/
Hunchback Of Notre Dame/I See Nothing
And Everything/Don't Judge Me
TJM Records TJE 101 September 1987

THE EARLY YEARS CD
Voice In The Dark/Every Day I Die/Passion/
Hunchback Of Notre Dame/See Nothing
And Everything/Don't Judge Me
Receiver Records, Receiver CD1 August 1990

RADIO SESSIONS

3 March 1981, Radio One, John Peel programme -
Ding-Dong/Searching For The Only One/Hunchback Of
Notre Dame/I Am The Man/Production Prevention

30 March 1981, Radio One, Richard Skinner
programme -Searching for the Only One/Hey! Hey!/
We Are Going Down/I Wish I Was King

30 September 1981, Radio One, John Peel
programme - And I Don't Care (Nobody Stays Here)/
After Hanging Around/What To Do?/I'm Not To See
Her/Ice Cream And Wafers

NB. * Merlin Records released a CD entitled 'Simply
Mick Hucknall' in 1992 (MER 004) which contained
the same six songs as 'The Early Years' albums.
*All copies of the single 'Voice In The Dark' had
blank white inner labels.
* The track 'Hunchback Of Notre Dame' was included
on the compilation of John Peel sessions, 'Manchester
So Much To Answer For' released in 1990 by Strange
Fruit Records (SFR202) on CD, vinyl and cassette.

SIMPLY RED

SINGLES

Money's Too Tight (To Mention)/Open Up
The Red Box
Elektra EKR 9 (7") June 1985

Money's Too Tight (To Mention)/Open Up
The Red Box/Every Bit Of Me
Elektra EKR 9T (12") June 1985

Money's Too Tight (To Mention)/Open Up
The Red Box
Elektra EKR 9P (7" picture disc) June 1985

Money's Too Tight (To Mention) (Special
Cutback Mix)/Open Up The Red Box
Elektra EKR 9TX (12") July 1985

Come To My Aid/Valentine
Elektra EKR 19 (7") September 1985

Come To My Aid (Extended)/Valentine/
Granma's Hands
Elektra EKR 19T (12") September 1985

Come To My Aid (Survival mix)/Granma's
Hands/Come To My Aid (Heavy Dub Mix)/
Valentine
Elektra EXR 19TX (12") September 1985

Holding Back The Years/I Won't Feel Bad
Elektra EKR 29 (7") November 1985

Holding Back The Years/I Won't Feel Bad/
Drowning In My Own Tears
Elektra EKR 29T (12") November 1985

Holding Back The Years/I Won't Feel Bad
Elektra EKR 29F (7" poster sleeve)
November 1985

Holding Back The Years/I Won't Feel Bad
Elektra EKR 29P (7" shaped picture disc)
November 1985

Jericho/Jericho (The Musical)
WEA YZ 63 (7") February 1986

Jericho/Jericho (The Musical)
WEA YZ 63C (7" red vinyl in transparent sleeve)
February 1986

Jericho/Jericho (The Musical)/Money's Too
Tight To Mention (live)/Heaven (live)
WEA YZ 63T (12") February 1986

Holding Back The Years/Drowning In My
Own Tears
WEA YZ 70 (7") June 1986

Holding Back The Years/ Drowning In My
Own Tears/Picture Book (Dub)
WEA YZ 70T (12") June 1986

Open Up The Red Box/ Look At You Now
WEA YZ 75 (7") August 1986

Open Up The Red Box (re-mix)/Look At You
Now/Heaven (live)
WEA YZ 75T (12") August 1986

Open Up The Red Box/Look At You Now
WEA YZ 75B (7" box sleeve) August 1986

Open Up The Red Box/Look At You Now
WEA YZ 75F (fold-out sleeve) August 1986

The Right Thing/There's A Light
WEA YZ 103 (7") February 1987

The Right Thing/There's A Light/Ev'ry Time
We Say Goodbye
WEA YZ 103T (12") February 1987

The Right Thing/There's A Light/Holding Back
The Years/Drowning In My Own Tears
WEA YZ 103F (7" double pack) February 1987

The Right Thing/There's A Light
WEA YZ 103V (7" fold out sleeve) February 1987

The Right Thing/There's A Light/Ev'ry Time
We Say Goodbye
WEA YZ 103TP (12" picture disc) February 1987

Infidelity/Lady Godiva's Room
WEA YZ 114 (7") May 1987

Infidelity (Stretch Mix)/Lady Godiva's Room/
Love Fire (Massive Red Mix)
WEA YZ 114T (12") May 1987

Infidelity (Stretch Mix)/Lady Godiva's Room/
Love Fire (Massive Red Mix)
WEA YZ 114P (12" picture disc) May 1987

Maybe Someday/Let Me Have It All (Re-mix) (7")
WEA YZ 141 (12" picture disc) July 1987

Maybe Someday/Let Me Have It All/Broken Man
WEA YZ 141T (12") July 1987

Ev'ry Time We Say Goodbye/Love For Sale (live)
WEA YZ 161 (7") November 1987

Ev'ry Time We Say Goodbye/Love For Sale
(live)/Ev'ry Time We Say Goodbye (live)
WEA YZ 161T (12") November 1987

Ev'ry Time We Say Goodbye/Love For Sale
(live)/Sad Old Red/Broken Man
WEA YZ 161CD (CD single) November 1987

Ev'ry Time We Say Goodbye/Love For Sale (live)/
Ev'ry Time We Say Goodbye (edit)
WEA YZ 161TX (12" postcard pack) November 1987

Ev'ry Time We Say Goodbye/Love For Sale (live)/
Sad Old Red/Broken Man
WEA YZ 161TE (10") November 1987

I Won't Feel Bad/Lady Godiva's Room
WEA YZ 172 (7") February 1988

I Won't Feel Bad (Arthur Baker re-mix)/
Lady Godiva's Room (Ellis Hucknall mix)/
I Won't Feel Bad (edit)
WEA YZ 172T (12") February 1988

I Won't Feel Bad (re-mix)/Lady Godiva's Room
(re-mix)/I Won't Feel Bad (edit)/The Right Thing
WEA YZ 172CD (CD single) February 1988

It's Only Love/Turn It Up
WEA YZ 349 (7") January 1989

It's Only Love
WEA YZ 349P (one-sided 7") January 1989

It's Only Love/Turn It Up/I'm Gonna Lose You
WEA YZ 349T (12") January 1989

It's Only Love/Turn It Up/The Right Thing/
I'm Gonna Lose You
WEA YZ 349CD (CD single) January 1989

It's Only Love (Valentine mix)/Turn It Up/
I'm Gonna Lose You
WEA YZ 349TE (10" numbered and limited
edition) February 1989

If You Don't Know Me By Now/Move On
Out (live)
WEA YZ 377 (7") April 1989

If You Don't Know Me By Now/Move On
Out (live)/Shine (live)
WEA 377T (12") April 1989

If You Don't Know Me By Now/Move On
Out (live)/Shine (live)/Sugar Daddy
WEA YZ 377CD (CD single) April 1989

If You Don't Know Me By Now/Move On
Out (live)/Shine (live)/Sugar Daddy
WEA YZ 377CDX (CD single in special package)
April 1989

If You Don't Know Me By Now/Move On
Out (live)/Great Divide
WEA YZ 377TE (10") April 1989

A New Flame/More
WEA YZ 404 (7") July 1989

A New Flame/More/I Asked Her For Water
(live)/Resume (live)
WEA YZ 404T (12") July 1989

A New Flame/More
WEA YZ 404C (cassette single) July 1989

A New Flame/More/I Asked Her For Water
(live)/Resume (live)
WEA YZ 404CD (CD single) July 1989

A New Flame/More/I Asked Her For Water
(live)/Funk On Out (live)
WEA YZ 404TE (10") July 1989

You've Got It/Holding Back The Years
(live acoustic version)
WEA YZ424 (7") October 1989

You've Got It/Holding Back The Years
(live acoustic version)
WEA YZ424TE (cassette single) October 1989

You've Got It/Holding Back The Years
(live acoustic)/I Wish
WEA YZ424T (12") October 1989

You've Got It/Holding Back The Years
(live acoustic)/I Wish/I Know You Got Soul
WEA YZ424TE (10") October 1989

You've Got It/Holding Back The Years
(live acoustic)/I Wish/I Know You Got Soul
WEA YZ424CD (3" CD) October 1989

Something Got Me Started/A New Flame
East West YZ614 (7") September 1991

Something Got Me Started/Something
Got Me Started (instrumental)/A New Flame
East West YZ614T (12") September 1991

Something Got Me Started/A New Flame
East West YZ614C (cassette single) September 1991

Something Got Me Started/Come On In My
Kitchen/A New Flame/Something Got Me Started
East West YZ614CD (CD single) September 1991

Stars/Stars (PM-IZED mix)
East West YZ626 (7") November 1991

Stars/Stars (PM-IZED mix)
East West YZ626C (cassette single) November 1991

Stars/Stars (Comprende mix)/Ramblin'
On My Mind/Something Got Me Started
(Hurley's House mix)
East West YZ626T (12") November 1991

Stars/Stars (Comprende mix)/Ramblin'
On My Mind/Something Got Me Started
(Hurley's House mix)
East West YZ626CD (CD single) November 1991

For Your Babies / For Your Babies
(Edition Français)
East West YZ642 (7") January 1992

For Your Babies/For Your Babies
(Edition Français)/Freedom (Perfecto mix)
East West YZ642T (12") January 1992

For Your Babies/For Your Babies
(Edition Français)
East West YZ642C (cassette single) January 1992

For Your Babies/For Your Babies (Edition
Français)/For Your Babies/Freedom
(How Long? mix)/Me And The Devil Blues
East West YZ642CD (CD single) January 1992

Thrill Me/Thrill Me (Nellee Cooper mix)
East West YZ671 (7") April 1992

Thrill Me/Thrill Me (Nellee Cooper mix)
East West YZ671C (cassette single) April 1992

Thrill Me (Connoisseur's mix)/
Thrill Me (Nellee Hooper's dub mix)/
Thrill Me (Stewart Levine's club mix)
East West YZ671T (12") April 1992

Thrill Me/Thrill Me (Nellee Hooper Mix)/
Thrill Me (live)/When You've Got A Friend
East West YZ671CD (CD single) April 1992

Your Mirror/Your Mirror (live)
East West YZ689 (7") July 1992

Your Mirror/Your Mirror (live)
East West YZ689C (cassette single) July 1992

Your Mirror/Sad Old Red (live)/She's
Got It Bad (live)
East West YZ689CD (CD single) July 1992

Your Mirror (live)/More (live)/Something
Got Me Started (live)
East West YZ689CDX (CD digipack single)
July 1992

MONTREUX EP - Love For Sale/
Granma's Hands/Drowning In My Own Tears/
Lady Godiva's Room
East West YZ716 (7" gatefold sleeve)
November 1992

MONTREUX EP - Love For Sale/
Granma's Hands/Drowning In My Own
Tears/Lady Godiva's Room
East West YZ716C (cassette single)
November 1992

MONTREUX EP - Love For Sale/
Granma's Hands/Drowning In My Own
Tears/Lady Godiva's Room
East West YZ716CD (jewel case CD)
November 1991

MONTREUX EP - Love For Sale/
Granma's Hands/Drowning In My Own
Tears/Lady Godiva's Room
East West YZ716CDX (digipack CD
with booklet) November 1991

NB. * The track 'Something's Burning' was included
on a flexi-disc given away with *Jamming!* magazine
in June 1985. Simply Red shared the flexi-disc with
10,000 Maniacs whose track was 'Grey Victory'.
* Simply Red's 'Every Bit Of Me' was featured on an
EP given away free with the short-lived *The Hit*
magazine in September 1985.

ALBUMS

PICTURE BOOK
Come To My Aid/ Sad Old Red/ Look At You
Now/ Heaven/ Jericho/ Money's Too Tight
(To Mention)/ Holding Back The Years/ Red Box/
No Direction/ Picture Book
Elektra EK27 October 1985

MEN AND WOMEN
The Right Thing/ Infidelity/ Suffer/ I Won't Feel Bad/
Ev'ry Time We Say Goodbye/ Let Me Have It All/ Love
Fire/ Move On Out/ Shine/ Maybe Someday...
WEA WX85 March 1987

A NEW FLAME
It's Only Love/ A New Flame/ You've Got It/
To Be With You/ More/ Turn It Up/ Love Lays Its
Tune/ She'll Have To Go/ If You Don't Know
Me By Now/ Enough
WEA WX242 February 1989

STARS
Something Got Me Started/ Stars/ Thrill Me/
Your Mirror/ She's Got It Bad/ For Your Babies/ Model/
How Could I Fall/ Freedom/ Wonderland
East West 9031-75284-2 October 1991

NB. Two Simply Red interview picture disc albums
have been released, in May 1987 (Baktabak BAK 2044)
and September 1988 (Tell Tales TT1001). A picture
disc version of 'Picture Book' was released (EKT27P).